riverstone kitchen
simple

riverstone kitchen
simple

Bevan Smith

Photography by Fiona Andersen

HarperCollins*Publishers*

contents

introduction

It has always been our belief that good food need not be complicated. Great ingredients, simply prepared, often make for the most memorable of meals. It's hard to deny the beauty in a succulent, ripe fig, or the lusciousness in a bowl of fat cherries; freshly dug new potatoes, just boiled and buttered; the garden's green beans — some of life's simple pleasures.

Since opening Riverstone Kitchen in November 2006, we continue to learn that nature is our greatest guide and our philosophy remains the same: all people should, and can, eat well. Eating seasonally makes complete sense, not only because it's better value but also for the simple fact that the food is fresher and tastier.

Developing our gardens has always been a priority, but little did we realize what an integral part of the restaurant the gardens would become. Now it seems almost inconceivable to not have these large productive gardens supporting and guiding us through each season. Striving to grow as much as is required in the day-to-day running of the business has been both challenging and rewarding but, most of all, it has strengthened our love and passion for growing things ourselves and it inspires us to share our knowledge with others. It is hugely satisfying to see the pleasure it brings to those who wander through the raised beds and orchards, and the beauty is that there is no reason why anyone can't achieve the same in their own backyard.

Wherever possible it has also been our objective to find the best ingredients available and, through our journey, we have discovered many local producers, often small, who are thoroughly committed to what they do, producing some outstanding products that could hold their own anywhere in the world. Supporting small producers is an easy choice for us because we believe everyone has both a responsibility and the ability to shape their community by the everyday ethical decisions they make.

When it comes to food, all regions have their own distinct identity with something unique to offer. In a country that is as young as New Zealand, we are well on the way to being able to express ourselves culturally through the food we cook and eat. Utilizing ingredients grown directly around us further defines who we are and what we have to offer region to region. Here at Riverstone Kitchen we do this on a daily basis and the focus on local produce has now become central to who we are and where we see ourselves in the future.

As the pace of modern life increases, a practical way of taking a step back and gaining some control over what we consume is to grow as much as we can of the everyday food we eat. That opportunity exists, regardless of where we live: whether it's a pot of herbs on the windowsill, a tray of micro-greens on the balcony or a trellis of staked beans against a garden wall, the simple pleasure gained from doing such things is considerable. The connection between people and the food we eat has never been more important. What we consume daily has a direct impact on our wellbeing and the motto 'healthier people make for healthier communities' rings as true as it ever did.

There has never been a better time to experience the diverse variety of food available to us today and, with the luxury of travel and technology, we literally have it all at our fingertips. Good food, however, will always be about where it comes from, how it is grown and how it is ultimately consumed. What is left for us to do is to remain true to ourselves and keep it, in the end, simple.

ingredients guide

To achieve great results in cooking we use the best ingredients possible. This is a guide to the ingredients we use in the following recipes.

chocolate — 53% for general cooking, 70% for bitter chocolate tarts

cocoa powder — Dutch cocoa powder

gelatine leaves — 4 gold-grade leaves per 500 ml liquid for firm set and 2½–3 leaves per 500 ml for soft set

Parmesan — Parmigiano Reggiano

parsley — Italian flat-leaf parsley

red wine vinegar — Forum Cabernet Sauvignon vinegar

risotto rice — Ferron Carnaroli for meat- or vegetable-based risotto and Ferron Vialone Nano for seafood risotto

salt — sea salt flakes (sea salt is emphasized to avoid over-seasoning with table salt)

truffle oil — Mas Portell black truffle oil

vanilla essence — real essence

kitchen essentials

8-inch mortar and pestle

Benriner Japanese vegetable slicer

Chinese spider — bamboo spoon (strainer)

electric mixer

electronic scales

food processor

heat-resistant rubber spatula

heavy-based stainless steel pots

large rolling pin

Microplane (fine zester or grater)

quality chef's knives — paring knife, bread knife, all-purpose cook's knife

quality ovenproof non-stick frying pan

solid cutting board

speed peeler

stainless steel mixing bowls

strong short-handled tongs

heatproof thermometer

breakfast

The most important meal of the day, breakfast, deserves more than just a passing thought. Get motivated and get off to a great start!

For those who love foraging for wild mushrooms in autumn, here is a recipe to make the most of your spoils.

wild mushrooms with garlic, parsley and lemon on sourdough

100 ml olive oil

4 handfuls fresh, wild, edible mushrooms (or Portobello mushrooms), sliced

salt and pepper

2 tbsp unsalted butter

4 slices sourdough bread (see page 189)

4 cloves garlic, peeled and crushed

½ cup parsley leaves, finely chopped

juice of 1 small lemon

2 cups rocket

serves 4

Heat half the olive oil in a large heavy-based frying pan over a high heat. When oil begins to smoke, add mushrooms, season with a little salt and pepper and fry for 30 seconds. Add remaining olive oil and butter to the pan once mushrooms have absorbed the initial oil. Continue to fry, cooking on all sides until liquid has disappeared and mushrooms are well coloured.

Lightly toast sourdough and divide between four plates. When mushrooms are cooked, add garlic and cook for a further 30 seconds before adding parsley and lemon juice. Toss together and serve on top of toasted sourdough. Finish with rocket and serve immediately.

IMPORTANT!
Check with a reliable source before picking and eating wild mushrooms. Some mushrooms are poisonous.

An old-school favourite, it's time to bring back the crumpet!

fresh crumpets with wild elderberry jelly

350 ml milk

2 tsp caster sugar

1 tsp dried yeast

360 g plain flour

1 pinch salt

½ tsp baking soda

200 ml water

2 tbsp unsalted butter

wild elderberry jelly, to serve (see page 199)

fresh cream, to serve (optional)

serves 4

Gently heat milk in a small pot until just warm. Place sugar, yeast, flour and salt in the bowl of an electric mixer with the warmed milk and beat to a smooth, firm batter.

Cover bowl with plastic wrap and allow to prove in a warm place for 1–1½ hours or until doubled in size.

Combine baking soda with the water and mix into batter on medium speed until smooth. Heat a large non-stick frying pan over a low heat. Add a knob of butter, then place six lightly greased 6 cm x 3 cm metal ring moulds in the pan. Spoon batter into moulds until half full. Cook for 4–5 minutes or until bubbles appear over the entire surface of the crumpets and a skin starts to form on the top. Remove rings and turn crumpets over in the pan until the tops have lightly coloured. Remove from pan and cool on a rack before cooking remaining crumpets.

Allow to cool for 5–10 minutes before serving with elderberry jelly and fresh cream, if desired.

Once you've smoked your own salmon, you'll never want to buy it again.

poached eggs with hot-smoked salmon and homemade butter

2 litres water

2 tbsp white vinegar

6 large free-range eggs

salt and pepper

240 g hot-smoked salmon
(see page 203)

1 tbsp finely chopped chives

40 g homemade butter
(see page 198)

6 slices ciabatta, toasted

serves 2

Heat the water in a large pot until boiling. Add vinegar and reduce heat to a simmer. Carefully crack eggs into water and lightly poach for 3 minutes or until just set and still soft. Remove eggs with a slotted spoon and drain on absorbent kitchen paper.

Divide eggs between two plates, lightly season with salt and pepper and serve immediately with hot-smoked salmon, chopped chives, homemade butter and toasted ciabatta.

The healthiest way to start your day.

muesli with fresh orange juice

3 cups rolled oats, lightly toasted

1 cup almonds, roughly chopped and lightly toasted

½ cup organic dried apricots, finely chopped

½ cup raisins

¼ cup goji berries

¼ cup shaved coconut, lightly toasted

¼ cup pumpkin seeds

¼ cup sunflower seeds

¼ cup chia seeds

1 tsp ground cinnamon

freshly squeezed orange juice, to serve

makes 500 g

Place all dry ingredients in a large bowl and mix well to combine. Store in an airtight container. To serve, place 1 cup muesli in a bowl with ½ cup freshly squeezed orange juice.

A gluten-free, dairy-free breakfast treat!

fig and almond bread with vanilla honey syrup

fig and almond bread

12 large dried figs, soaked in water overnight

2½ cups ground almonds

6 free-range eggs

2 tsp baking powder

½ cup loosely packed brown sugar

1 tsp vanilla essence

8 fresh figs, halved, to serve

1 cup vanilla honey syrup (see below), to serve

serves 8

Preheat oven to 180°C. Line an 8 cm x 20 cm loaf tin with baking paper. Place the first six ingredients in a food processor and blend until smooth. Pour into prepared loaf tin and cook for 20–25 minutes or until a skewer comes out clean. Leave to cool in pan before turning out and serving with fresh figs and vanilla honey syrup.

vanilla honey syrup

1 cup caster sugar

¾ cup water

½ tsp vanilla bean paste

3 tbsp honey

makes 1½ cups

Place sugar, water and vanilla paste in a small saucepan and bring to the boil over a medium to high heat. Remove from heat and stir in honey until dissolved. Allow to cool completely.

Store in an airtight container in the refrigerator for up to one month.

Free-range eggs, tasty cheese and fresh herbs — the perfect omelette every time.

cheese and herb omelette

5 large free-range eggs

¼ tsp salt

2 pinches black pepper

2 tbsp unsalted butter

1 cup Maasdam cheese, grated

1 spring onion, finely chopped

2 tbsp parsley leaves, chopped

1 tbsp finely chopped chives

4 slices wholegrain toast, to serve

serves 2

Place eggs, salt and pepper in a large stainless steel bowl and whisk well. Heat a non-stick frying pan over a medium heat, add butter and, once butter has melted and begins to sizzle, pour in eggs and cook, without stirring, until omelette starts to set. Sprinkle with cheese, spring onion and herbs and continue to cook for a further 20 seconds. Using a plastic egg flip, gently loosen the edges of the omelette around the pan. Once omelette is two-thirds cooked, fold in half and slide from the pan onto a large plate. Cut in half and serve immediately on two plates with wholegrain toast on the side.

A strong coffee and a good pastry — a great way to start the day!

cherry almond tarts

300 g puff pastry
(see page 193)

50 g unsalted butter, softened

50 g caster sugar

50 g ground almonds

10 g plain flour

1 large free-range egg

¼ tsp vanilla essence

36 whole cherries, pitted

caster sugar, to dust

icing sugar, to serve

serves 6

Preheat oven to 200°C. Line an oven tray with baking paper. Roll puff pastry out until 4–5 mm thick. Cut six 10 cm rounds from pastry using a large cookie cutter. Place rounds on oven tray.

Place butter, sugar, almonds, flour, egg and vanilla essence in a food processor and blend to a smooth paste. Spoon 1 tbsp almond paste onto each pastry round and spread out evenly leaving a 1 cm border around the edges. Place 6 cherries on each tart and dust heavily with caster sugar.

Bake for 20–25 minutes or until pastry is very crisp and golden brown. Remove from oven and allow to cool before serving. Dust with icing sugar, if desired.

Something the whole family can make.

toasted banana bread
with maple syrup

¼ cup milk

¼ cup olive oil

½ cup maple syrup

1 tsp vanilla extract

4 large ripe bananas

2 cups wholemeal flour, sifted

1 tsp baking powder, sifted

1 tsp baking soda, sifted

1 cup rolled oats

1 pinch salt

½ cup sliced almonds

½ cup chia seeds or pumpkin seeds

extra banana, to serve

extra maple syrup, to serve

makes one 10 cm x 20 cm loaf

Preheat oven to 180°C. Line a 10 cm x 20 cm loaf tin with baking paper.

Place milk, olive oil, maple syrup, vanilla extract and bananas in a food processor and blend until smooth. In a large bowl, combine flour, baking powder, baking soda, oats, salt, almonds and chia or pumpkin seeds. Add banana mixture to dry ingredients and combine, mixing as little as possible.

Pour into prepared loaf tin and bake for 45 minutes or until golden brown and a skewer comes out clean. Remove from oven and allow to cool slightly before turning out onto a cooling rack. Once cool, slice and toast banana bread before serving with fresh banana and maple syrup.

Who can resist fried eggs Spanish-style?

fried free-range eggs with chorizo, potatoes and salsa rossa

2 fresh chorizos

60 ml olive oil

2 medium Agria potatoes, cooked and sliced

6 free-range eggs

1 pinch Spanish sweet-smoked paprika

2 tbsp parsley leaves, roughly chopped

1 cup salsa rossa, warmed
(see page 197)

serves 2

Preheat oven to 180°C. Place chorizos in a small pot of water and bring to a simmer over a medium heat. Remove pot from heat and allow chorizos to cool in cooking liquor. Once cold, slice into 1 cm-thick slices and set aside.

Heat olive oil in a large heavy-based ovenproof frying pan over a high heat and fry sliced potatoes until golden on both sides. Add chorizo slices and colour on both sides. Crack eggs into pan and cook for 20 seconds before placing frying pan in oven for 2–3 minutes or until eggs are just cooked.

Remove pan from oven and sprinkle with paprika and parsley. Divide between two plates, spoon warmed salsa rossa over the top and serve immediately.

Seldom has breakfast tasted so good!

roast peaches, toasted panettone and natural yoghurt

6 ripe peaches, halved with stones removed

80 g caster sugar

¼ tsp vanilla bean paste

8 slices panettone

1 cup natural yoghurt

icing sugar, to dust

serves 4

Preheat oven to 200°C. Place peaches on a baking paper-lined oven tray. Mix sugar and vanilla paste together in a small bowl until vanilla is evenly mixed through.

Dredge peaches with the vanilla sugar and roast for 15–20 minutes until tender and sugar starts to caramelize. Remove from oven and allow to cool slightly.

Place panettone on a baking tray and lightly grill on both sides until golden brown. (Be careful, as panettone colours quickly.)

Divide panettone and peaches between four plates and finish with natural yoghurt and remaining roast peach juices. Dust with icing sugar and serve immediately.

Forget bland shop-bought imitations. These are the real deal.

hot cross buns

1 cup raisins

¾ cup currants

zest and juice of 1 orange

800 g plain flour

525 ml lukewarm water

10 g dried yeast

10 g salt

½ cup soft brown sugar

1 tsp ground cinnamon

1 tsp mixed spice

½ tsp ground nutmeg

1 tsp ground allspice

½ cup mixed peel

2 tbsp olive oil

½ cup plain flour, for crosses

¾ cup bun glaze (see below)

makes 12

Place raisins, currants, and orange zest and juice in a stainless steel bowl and soak overnight.

Place soaked fruit, flour, water, yeast, salt, sugar, spices, mixed peel and olive oil in the bowl of an electric mixer with dough hook attachment. Mix on low speed for 15 minutes, then turn out into another large bowl, lightly greased with a little more olive oil. Cover bowl with plastic wrap and set aside in a warm place until doubled in size. Turn dough out onto a clean bench top and divide into 12 equal pieces. Knead each piece of dough into a ball and place each ball 1 cm apart on a baking paper-lined oven tray. Cover buns with a tea towel, return to a warm place and allow to prove for a further 30–45 minutes or until almost doubled in size.

Preheat oven to 200°C. To make crosses, mix flour with a little water to make a thick paste. Place in a piping bag and pipe a thin cross onto each bun.

Place buns in oven and cook for 15–20 minutes or until golden brown. Remove from oven and brush with bun glaze. Allow to cool before serving.

bun glaze

½ cup sugar

¼ cup water

makes ¾ cup

Place sugar and water in a small pot over a medium to high heat. Bring to the boil and stir until sugar is dissolved. Remove from heat and allow to cool slightly before using.

lunch

The perfect excuse to catch up with friends! A long, lazy lunch or a fast bite for those on the go — keep it quick and easy to make more time for the important things.

Light, fresh and bursting with flavour — everything a good lunch should be.

free-range chicken salad with quinoa, grapes, basil and verjuice

1 cup quinoa

2 cups water

salt and pepper

2 cloves garlic, crushed

3 cups basil leaves, washed

60 ml olive oil

4 free-range chicken breasts, skin on

100 ml extra virgin olive oil

100 ml verjuice

3 cups seedless grapes, halved

4 cups baby lettuce leaves

serves 4

Rinse quinoa under cold running water through a fine sieve. Place in a small saucepan with the water and bring to the boil over a high heat. Turn off heat, place lid on pot and allow to steam for 20–30 minutes or until tender. Set aside.

Preheat oven to 200°C. Place ½ tsp salt, half the garlic and ½ cup basil in a mortar and grind to a paste. Add 30 ml olive oil and muddle. Spread paste under the skin of the chicken and season chicken with salt and pepper. Place skin-side down in a hot, heavy-based ovenproof frying pan with the remaining 30 ml olive oil. Fry until skin turns a golden brown, then place frying pan in oven and roast chicken for 5–6 minutes or until almost cooked. Carefully remove from oven, turn chicken over and allow to rest in the pan, skin-side up. The remaining heat in the pan will continue the cooking process.

In a saucepan, gently warm the extra virgin olive oil over a medium heat. Add remaining garlic and cook for 30 seconds without colouring, before adding verjuice and grapes. Remove from heat and add any resting juices from the chicken to the saucepan.

Place lettuce and remaining basil in a large bowl with the quinoa. Slice chicken and add to the bowl. Toss together with the verjuice and grape dressing, season to taste with a little salt and pepper and divide between four plates. Serve immediately.

The clean flavours of sweet, sour, salty and hot —
the essence of Thai food.

seared squid with pomelo and tamarind

500 g squid tubes

1½ cups pomelo flesh

¼ red onion, finely sliced

2 spring onions, finely sliced

1 cup coriander leaves, washed

½ cup mint leaves, washed

1 cup basil leaves, washed

12–16 nasturtium leaves

2 long red chillies, seeds removed and finely sliced

¼ lime, finely chopped with skin on

50 ml peanut oil

1 cup tamarind dressing
(see page 200)

serves 4

Slice squid tubes in half, remove any internal membranes and score diagonally along the inner sides. Place the pomelo, red onion, spring onion, herbs, nasturtium leaves, chilli and lime in a large mixing bowl and lightly toss together.

In batches, heat peanut oil in a large non-stick frying pan over a very high heat and cook squid quickly, scored-side down, for 1 minute. Turn squid over and cook for a further 30 seconds. Remove from pan and set aside.

Once squid is cooked, add to salad with half the tamarind dressing and gently toss together. Divide between four plates and finish with remaining dressing. Serve immediately.

In summer, this is as good as life gets!

salad of prosciutto, cherries, goat's curd and vincotto

100 g prosciutto, very thinly sliced

32 ripe cherries, pitted

2 cups rocket leaves

150 g goat's curd

4 tbsp vincotto

2 tbsp extra virgin olive oil

serves 4

Divide prosciutto between four plates and scatter with cherries and rocket. Crumble goat's curd over the top and drizzle with vincotto and olive oil. Serve immediately.

While I love everything about zucchini, the plants themselves do have a tendency to produce much more than you usually need. A great way to keep rampant zucchini under control is by picking the flowers — both male and female — and stuffing them with a combination of cheeses. Deep-fried in a light batter until crisp, they are absolutely fantastic and are always a hit with diners when they're on the menu.

Zucchini flowers can also be stuffed with seafood, and steamed or chopped up and eaten in pasta and salads. They are seldom seen for sale to the public as they have an extremely short shelf life, so treat yourself to this delicate delight and simply grow your own.

The most delicious way to keep any zucchini patch under control.

deep-fried zucchini flowers with four cheeses

150 g fresh ricotta

70 g mascarpone

50 g blue cheese, crumbled

40 g Parmesan, grated

8 zucchini flowers

2 litres sunflower or canola oil

chickpea batter (see below)

salt

2 cups micro-greens

1 lemon, quartered

serves 4

Mix cheeses together in a bowl until well combined. Gently place a generous spoonful of cheese mixture into each zucchini flower and set aside. Heat oil in a large heavy-based pot over a medium to high heat until oil reaches 170°C. (Use a heatproof thermometer to test the oil temperature.) Dip stuffed zucchini flowers into chickpea batter until fully coated, then carefully place in the oil and fry for 2 minutes on each side until crisp and golden. Remove from pot with a slotted spoon and drain on absorbent paper. Season with a little salt and serve immediately with micro-greens and lemon.

chickpea batter

½ cup cornflour

½ cup chickpea flour

1 tsp salt

¼ tsp ground black pepper

150 ml soda water

2 free-range egg whites

Place all dry ingredients in a large bowl. Add soda water and whisk to a smooth batter. In a separate bowl, whisk egg whites to a soft peak, then gently fold into the batter.

Picking crab takes time, but it's well worth the effort for good crab mayo.

crab mayonnaise with sourdough, salad greens and lemon

300 g fresh, picked crab meat
(approximately 6–8 whole paddle crabs)

3 tbsp fresh mayonnaise
(see page 196)

¼ cup chives, finely chopped

¼ cup parsley leaves, finely chopped

2 tbsp fennel herb, finely chopped

salt and pepper

1 cup parsley leaves, washed

1 cup baby spinach

1 cup rocket

¼ small red onion, finely sliced

2 spring onions, finely sliced

2 tbsp lemon wholegrain mustard
dressing (see page 199)

4 slices sourdough bread
(see page 189)

1 lemon, quartered

serves 4

Place picked crab in a stainless steel bowl with mayonnaise, chives, parsley and fennel. Lightly mix together and season to taste with a little salt and pepper. Divide between four plates. Place remaining salad ingredients in a separate bowl with the lemon wholegrain mustard dressing and toss together. Serve salad on the side with sourdough and lemon wedges.

Thai chicken salad with coconut, chilli and roasted peanuts

1 x 400 ml can good-quality coconut cream

2 free-range skinless chicken breasts

1 tsp sea salt

2 pinches dried chilli flakes

3 cloves garlic, peeled

50 g palm sugar, crushed with a mortar and pestle

juice of 4 limes (or juice of 1½ lemons)

3 tsp fish sauce

2 cups baby spinach leaves

1 fresh red chilli, seeds removed and finely sliced

½ cup mint leaves, washed and roughly torn

¼ cup Vietnamese mint leaves (optional)

1 cup coriander leaves, washed

½ cup basil leaves, roughly torn

¼ red onion, finely sliced

1 cup finely sliced (Asian-style) spring onions

3 tbsp deep-fried shallots (available from Asian supermarkets)

¼ cup blanched peanuts, roasted and roughly chopped

1 tbsp chive flowers (optional)

serves 4

Place coconut cream and chicken breasts in a small stainless steel pot and bring to the boil over a medium to high heat. Reduce heat to low and simmer for 5–6 minutes or until chicken is cooked. Remove pot from heat and allow chicken to cool in the coconut liquor. Once cool, remove chicken from pot, reserving coconut liquor, and shred chicken into fine strips using your fingers. Refrigerate chicken until ready to assemble salad.

Grind sea salt and chilli flakes together in a mortar. Add garlic and continue to grind to a smooth paste. Place paste and reserved coconut liquor in a small pot and bring to the boil over a medium to high heat. Add palm sugar, remove from heat and stir with a wooden spoon until sugar is dissolved. Add lime juice and fish sauce and adjust seasoning with a little more fish sauce, if desired. Refrigerate until completely cool.

To assemble salad, place baby spinach, red chilli, mint, coriander, basil, red onion, spring onions and shredded chicken in a large mixing bowl. Add 3–4 tbsp coconut dressing and lightly toss together. Divide between four plates, drizzle with a little of the remaining dressing to taste and finish with deep-fried shallots, roasted peanuts and chive flowers, if desired.

About as simple as it gets, these are an absolute staff favourite!

fish cakes with sweet chilli sauce

200 g uncooked prawn tails, shelled, deveined and coarsely chopped

300 g white fish fillets, bones removed and coarsely chopped

100 g smoked salmon, coarsely chopped

1 x 4 cm knob fresh ginger, peeled and grated

5 cloves garlic, peeled and crushed

2 red chillies, seeds removed and finely sliced

zest and juice of 2 limes

3 tsp fish sauce

3 cups coriander leaves, washed

60 ml peanut oil

¼ small red onion, finely sliced

1 cup basil leaves, washed

½ cup mint leaves, washed

¼ cup Vietnamese mint leaves, washed (optional)

1½ cups finely sliced spring onions

1 tbsp cold water

1 cup sweet chilli sauce (see page 197)

serves 4

Preheat oven to 180°C. Place prawns, fish and salmon in a large bowl with ginger, garlic, chilli, lime zest and juice and fish sauce. Roughly chop half the coriander, add to the bowl and mix together well. Mould 3 tbsp fish cake mixture into small rounds, about 5–6 cm in diameter, squeezing well to bond the mix together. Flatten fish cakes with a spatula until 1 cm thick and place on a baking paper-lined oven tray, lightly greased with canola spray to prevent sticking.

Heat a little of the peanut oil in a large non-stick frying pan over a medium to high heat. When oil starts to smoke, cook fish cakes in batches for 1 minute on each side. Place cooked fish cakes on another baking paper-lined oven tray, then place in oven for 2 minutes to bring back up to temperature and to finish the cooking process before serving.

Remove fish cakes from oven and divide between four plates. Place salad ingredients in a large bowl and toss together gently with the cold water before serving next to the fish cakes. Drizzle a little chilli sauce over fish cakes and serve with a little extra sauce on the side, if desired. Serve immediately.

Superbly fresh tuna deserves respect and, as such, needs only to be quickly seared and sliced, or simply served raw.

seared tuna with pickled cucumber and sesame

50 ml peanut oil

400 g fresh tuna, trimmed and cut into 4 pieces, lengthways

1 tsp salt

1 cup pickled cucumber (see below)

2 tsp black and white sesame seeds, lightly toasted

¼ tsp Sichuan pepper salt (see page 203)

½ cup wild sorrel or micro-greens

1 large red chilli, seeds removed and finely diced

2 tbsp tamari

serves 4

Heat peanut oil in a large non-stick frying pan over a very high heat. Season tuna with salt. When oil begins to smoke, carefully place tuna pieces in pan and sear for 10–15 seconds on each side. Remove tuna from pan and allow to rest for 1 minute before slicing.

Divide tuna between four plates, dress with pickled cucumber and sprinkle with sesame seeds and Sichuan pepper salt. Finish with salad greens, chilli and a drizzle of tamari to taste.

pickled cucumber

½ cup liquid honey

½ cup water

½ cup white wine vinegar

1 telegraph cucumber, cut into small cubes

makes 3 cups

Place honey, water and vinegar in a small saucepan and bring to the boil over a medium to high heat. Remove from heat, add cucumber and allow to cool. Once cool, store in an airtight container in the refrigerator for up to three weeks.

seared scallops with green apple, roasted macadamia nuts and curry dressing

2 cups baby lettuce, washed

1 medium Granny Smith apple, finely sliced then cut into matchsticks

50 g macadamia nuts, roasted

2 spring onions, finely sliced

25 ml olive oil

200 g scallops

15 g unsalted butter

½ tsp lemon juice

100 ml curry dressing (see below)

serves 2

Place lettuce, apple, macadamia nuts and spring onions in a large bowl and toss together. Heat olive oil in a non-stick frying pan over a high heat until oil just begins to smoke. Sear scallops for 20 seconds on each side before adding butter and lemon juice and tossing to combine. Immediately remove scallops from the pan and place in the bowl with salad ingredients and half the curry dressing. Gently toss the salad and divide between two plates. Finish with a little extra dressing and serve immediately.

curry dressing

1 small green apple, peeled, cored and roughly chopped

½ small brown onion, roughly chopped

1 cup grape seed or sunflower oil

2 tsp curry powder

1 pinch dried chilli flakes

1 tsp ground turmeric

juice of ½ lemon

salt and pepper

makes 1½ cups

Place apple, onion and ¼ cup oil in a small saucepan and cook without colouring for 5 minutes or until onion and apple are soft and translucent. Add curry powder, chilli flakes and turmeric and cook for a further minute before adding remaining oil. Reduce temperature to low and gently warm dressing for 10–15 minutes. Remove from heat and allow to cool before blending in a food processor. Finish with lemon juice, and season with a little salt and pepper to taste.

A classic from Philip Johnson's e'cco bistro in Brisbane, this dish represents everything I liked and learnt about Philip's approach to food during my time there.

Parmesan tart with red onion jam

½ cup red onion jam (see page 201)

1 recipe savoury short crust pastry, blind baked (see page 191)

1 tbsp thyme leaves, finely chopped

8 free-range eggs

800 ml cream

150 g ground Parmesan

¼ cup parsley leaves, roughly chopped

½ tsp salt

¼ tsp pepper

salad greens, to serve

serves 9

Preheat oven to 160°C. Spread red onion jam evenly over the bottom of cooked tart case and sprinkle with thyme. Whisk eggs, cream, Parmesan, parsley, salt and pepper together and pour into tart case. Bake for 50–60 minutes or until just set. Remove from oven and allow to cool completely.

Cut into nine wedges, reheat for 5 minutes in a 200°C oven and serve with salad greens.

Shellfish and pasta — once again, the Italians have got it right!

Blueskin Bay clams with capellini, tomato and oregano

900 g fresh clams

160 g capellini pasta, cooked al dente

80 ml extra virgin olive oil

½ head garlic, peeled and finely chopped

500 g mixed coloured tomatoes, halved

½ cup oregano leaves, roughly chopped

salt and pepper

serves 2

Place clams in a large bowl of cold water for 1 hour to purge any residual sand. Drain, rinse under running water and set aside. Reheat cooked pasta in a medium-sized pot of simmering water. Remove from heat and drain. Heat half the olive oil in a large heavy-based pot before adding clams and placing a lid on top. Cook for 2 minutes until shells begin to open, then add garlic and tomatoes. Shake pot well to mix everything together and cook for a further minute. Remove from heat, add pasta and oregano and stir to combine. Adjust seasoning to taste with a little salt and pepper, divide between two bowls and serve immediately.

Undeniably delicious, and just perfect for lunch.

penne with broad beans, mint and sole

3 cups broad beans, podded

1 clove garlic, peeled and finely chopped

1 cup parsley leaves, finely chopped

zest and juice of 1 lemon

100 ml extra virgin olive oil

½ cup ground Parmesan

salt and pepper

50 ml olive oil

500 g sole fillets, cut into 3 cm pieces

200 g penne pasta, cooked al dente

½ cup mint leaves, washed

serves 4

Place broad beans and garlic in a food processor and blend until smooth. Add parsley, lemon zest and juice, extra virgin olive oil and half the Parmesan and blend to combine. Season to taste with a little salt and pepper and reserve for later use.

Heat some olive oil in a large non-stick frying pan over a high heat. Season sole with a little salt and pepper and fry in batches for 30 seconds until almost cooked. Remove from pan and reserve in a large stainless steel bowl. Warm broad bean purée in the same pan before adding to the sole. Reheat penne in a large pot of boiling water, drain well and gently mix with sole and broad bean purée. Finely chop mint and fold through pasta before dividing between four bowls and finishing with remaining Parmesan. Serve immediately.

Cavolo nero is one of our favourite brassicas. Easy to grow and extremely hardy, it seems to thrive almost year-round, making it a real mainstay in the garden — especially through the long, cold winter months when most other fresh greens struggle. Firm in texture, the young leaves are remarkably tender, either blanched or quickly stir-fried in a little olive oil. Perfect on its own or as an accompaniment to both meat and fish, cavolo nero is loved by gardeners and cooks alike.

Rustic country eating at its best!

roast quail with wet polenta, cavolo nero and salmoriglio

¼ tsp salt

1 cup oregano leaves, washed

½ clove garlic

zest of ½ lemon

100 ml olive oil

1 recipe wet polenta (see page 195)

50 ml milk

4 large quails, butterflied

salt and pepper

1 bunch cavolo nero, stalks removed

120 ml jus, warmed (see page 204)

serves 4

Bring a large pot of salted water to the boil over a high heat. To make salmoriglio, place salt in a mortar with the oregano and garlic and grind to a smooth paste. Add lemon zest and half the olive oil. Muddle together and reserve.

Warm wet polenta and milk in a small pot over a medium heat. Remove from heat and keep warm.

Lightly season quails with a little salt and pepper. Heat remaining olive oil in a heavy-based frying pan over a high heat. When oil begins to smoke, place quails, skin-side down, in the pan and cook for 3 minutes before turning and cooking for a further minute. Remove quails from pan and keep warm.

Blanch cavolo nero for 1 minute in boiling water before draining and squeezing out excess water.

Divide wet polenta and cavolo nero between four plates, halve quails and place on top. Finish with jus and a drizzle of salmoriglio. Serve immediately.

Quintessential comfort food that's hard to resist.

free-range chicken and vegetable pies

50 ml olive oil

salt and pepper

3 free-range chicken breasts, skin removed and cut into large pieces

1 medium carrot, peeled and chopped

½ head garlic, peeled and roughly chopped

1 onion, peeled and roughly chopped

1 stalk celery, roughly chopped

1 tbsp unsalted butter

500 ml chicken stock (see page 205)

2 tbsp parsley leaves, chopped

1 tbsp thyme leaves, finely chopped

3 tbsp cornflour

½ cup cold water

300 g pie base pastry (see page 193)

300 g puff pastry (see page 193)

1 free-range egg, beaten

makes 4 pies

Heat olive oil in a heavy-based saucepan over a medium to high heat. Season chicken pieces and fry for 1–2 minutes. Remove from pan and set aside. Add vegetables and butter to the pan and sweat over a medium heat for 10 minutes without colouring until vegetables start to soften. Add chicken stock and bring to the boil. Add chicken, parsley and thyme, adjust seasoning to taste with a little salt and pepper and reduce heat to low. Mix cornflour with the cold water and add to pie filling. Simmer for 2–3 minutes until pie filling thickens. Remove from heat, pour into a roasting tray and cool in the refrigerator until completely cold.

Preheat oven to 200°C. To prepare pie cases, unwrap pie base pastry and roll out on a lightly floured bench top to a 30 cm x 30 cm square, 3–4 mm thick. Place four 10 cm round pie tins on a baking tray. Drape pie base pastry sheet over pie tins. Gently press pastry into each pie tin, leaving pastry in one piece. Remove pie filling from refrigerator and spoon into each pie case. Brush the pastry lip of each pie with a little cold water.

To prepare pie tops, roll out puff pastry on a lightly floured bench top to a 30 cm x 30 cm square, 3–4 mm thick. Drape over pies and gently press down on the edge of each pie tin to seal the top and bottom, then cut extra pastry away from the side. Remove excess pastry and brush pie tops with beaten egg. Place in the refrigerator for 15 minutes to allow pastry to rest.

Bake for 20 minutes until pastry is a deep golden brown. Remove from oven and allow to cool slightly before serving.

honey-glazed ham on sourdough with aged Cheddar, mustard mayo and chow-chow

8 slices fresh sourdough bread
(see page 189)

1 cup mayonnaise (see page 196)

2 tsp wholegrain mustard

8 lettuce leaves

4 slices aged Cheddar

8 slices honey-glazed ham (see below)

1 cup chow-chow (see page 201)

serves 4

Lay slices of sourdough on a bread board. Mix mayonnaise and wholegrain mustard in a small bowl and spread 1 tbsp mustard mayonnaise on each slice of sourdough. Divide lettuce between four slices of sourdough, then top with slices of cheese and ham and finally a couple of healthy spoonfuls of chow-chow. Top each sandwich with a final layer of sourdough and serve.

honey-glazed ham

1 leg ham on bone, cooked and
skin removed

2 cups brown sugar

1 cup liquid honey

1 litre pineapple juice

Preheat oven to 200°C. Place ham in a large roasting dish. Place sugar, honey and pineapple juice in a large heavy-based saucepan and bring to the boil. Reduce by half, then pour over prepared ham. Cook for 20–30 minutes, basting frequently. Remove when ham is dark golden in colour and glaze is completely reduced.

The tasty solution to an age-old farming dilemma!

wild rabbit kebabs with flatbread and pear and walnut chutney

2 whole wild rabbits, skinned, gutted, hung and aged for 3–4 days in the refrigerator

4 cloves garlic, peeled and crushed

2 tbsp thyme leaves, finely chopped

zest of 1 lemon

150 ml olive oil

20 kebab sticks

salt and pepper

2 cups pear and walnut chutney (see page 202)

20 flatbreads, warmed (see page 191)

2 cups salad greens

Tabasco sauce, to finish (optional)

serves 4

Bone rabbits and cut meat into 1–2 cm pieces. Place in a medium-sized bowl with garlic, thyme, lemon zest and half the olive oil. Toss together to combine, then skewer meat onto 20 kebab sticks, cover with plastic wrap and refrigerate overnight.

Preheat oven to 180°C. Heat half the remaining olive oil in a large heavy-based frying pan over a high heat and cook kebabs in batches, for 1 minute on each side, until almost cooked. Place kebabs on a baking tray and place in oven for 2 minutes to finish cooking. Spoon a little pear and walnut chutney onto each flatbread, place a rabbit kebab on top and remove stick. Sprinkle with a few salad greens and serve with a couple of dashes of Tabasco sauce, if desired.

TIP
Like all wild game, rabbit benefits from hanging for 3–4 days before cooking, to help tenderize the meat.

platters

Small bursts of flavour — a great way to get any party started in style.

A classic flavour combination that never fails.

pumpkin, feta and sage on crostini

½ butternut pumpkin, skin and seeds removed, cut into 3 cm pieces

150 ml olive oil

1½ tsp ground cumin

½ tsp salt

¼ tsp pepper

½ baguette, sliced into 20 x 8 mm slices

½ cup fresh sage leaves, washed

100 g feta, crumbled

makes 20 canapés

Preheat oven to 180°C. Place pumpkin on a baking paper-lined oven tray and drizzle with 100 ml olive oil. Season with cumin, salt and pepper, cover with aluminium foil and roast for 30 minutes or until pumpkin begins to soften. Discard foil, return to oven and continue to roast for a further 5 minutes. Remove from oven and allow to cool.

To make crostini, place bread slices on an oven tray and drizzle with remaining olive oil. Bake for 3–4 minutes until the edges begin to turn golden brown. Remove from oven and allow to cool.

Finely chop sage and place in a mixing bowl with feta and roast pumpkin. Mix lightly together and season with a little extra salt and pepper, if required. Spoon pumpkin mixture onto each crostini and serve immediately.

There is nothing more satisfying than a plump, juicy, red tomato, vine-ripened and picked in the sun. Ever popular, there are literally hundreds of varieties available, from heirloom to hybrid and in all manner of colours, shapes and sizes, meaning versatility and interest in the kitchen.

Summer is, of course, when tomatoes are at their absolute best, so it makes sense to grow them alongside other summer favourites, like basil and parsley, to make the most of these classic combinations. For the best flavour, allow tomatoes to ripen on the vine and, once harvested, never store in the refrigerator as it changes the flavour and texture of this terrific fruit.

Fresh buffalo mozzarella is a real treat. Matched with ripe tomatoes and basil, you can't go wrong.

buffalo mozzarella with tomato, basil and black olive tapenade

¼ loaf sourdough bread
(see page 189)

1 tbsp olive oil

3–4 ripe medium-sized acid-free tomatoes, sliced into 20 pieces

salt and pepper

20 basil leaves, washed

1 large ball fresh buffalo mozzarella, sliced into 20 pieces

2 tbsp black olive tapenade

1 tbsp extra virgin olive oil

makes 20 canapés

Preheat oven to 180°C. Thinly slice sourdough into 20 pieces, each 3–4 cm in size, place on an oven tray and drizzle with olive oil. Bake for 3–4 minutes then remove from oven and allow to cool. Place a slice of tomato on each crostini and season with a little salt and pepper. Place a basil leaf on each slice of tomato, followed by a piece of mozzarella. Mix tapenade with extra virgin olive oil in a small bowl and drizzle over mozzarella. Place on a platter and serve immediately.

Quick, easy and elegant for stress-free entertaining.

hot-smoked salmon and crème fraîche on crostini

½ loaf ciabatta or baguette, sliced into 20 x 8 mm slices

40 ml olive oil

¾ cup crème fraîche

100 g hot-smoked salmon (see page 203)

¼ cup parsley leaves, finely chopped

2 tbsp finely chopped chives

1 tbsp fennel herb, picked and finely chopped

salt and pepper

2 heads chive flowers, picked (optional)

makes 20 canapés

Preheat oven to 180°C. To make crostini, place bread slices on an oven tray and drizzle with olive oil. Bake for 3–4 minutes until the edges begin to turn golden brown. Remove from oven and allow to cool. Place crème fraîche, salmon, parsley, chives and fennel in a bowl and gently combine. Season to taste with a little salt and pepper and spoon onto crostini. Finish with chive flowers, if desired, and serve immediately.

Balance, texture and flavour — the hallmarks of a great canapé.

crisp bacon, blue cheese, pear and balsamic

4–5 slices streaky bacon

1 ripe pear, cut into small, fine slices

100 g strong blue cheese, crumbled into small pieces

¼ cup parsley leaves, washed

1 tbsp finely sliced red onion

20 ml balsamic vinegar

20 ml extra virgin olive oil

makes 20 canapés

Grill bacon until crisp, drain on absorbent kitchen paper, then roughly chop into small pieces. Place 20 Chinese spoons on a tray and place a piece of bacon on each spoon. Continue to build canapés by alternately placing pieces of pear, blue cheese, parsley, onion and remaining bacon carefully on each spoon. Drizzle each spoon with a few drops of balsamic vinegar and finish with extra virgin olive oil. Place spoons on a platter and serve immediately.

Make it hot and spicy with this delicious Thai starter.

prawn with chilli, garlic and coriander

1 long red chilli, cut in half, seeds removed and finely sliced

12 large cooked prawns, peeled, deveined and roughly chopped

1 cup coriander leaves, washed

½ cup basil leaves, washed

½ cup finely sliced spring onions

1 tbsp finely sliced red onion

20 medium-sized English spinach leaves

½ cup Thai dressing (see below)

2 tbsp deep-fried shallots (available from Asian supermarkets)

makes 20 canapés

Place chilli, prawns, coriander, basil, spring onion and red onion in a large bowl and lightly toss together. Lay spinach leaves on a tray and place a small amount of prawn salad on each leaf. Dress each canapé with a little Thai dressing and finish with a sprinkle of deep-fried shallots. Carefully transfer each canapé to a platter and serve immediately.

Thai dressing

1 long red chilli, seeds removed and roughly chopped

½ tsp salt

1 clove garlic, peeled

50 g palm sugar

zest of 1 lime

juice of 2 limes

2 tsp fish sauce

makes ½ cup

Place chilli, salt and garlic in a mortar and grind to a smooth paste. Add palm sugar and crush into the paste. Add lime zest, juice and fish sauce and muddle. Store dressing in an airtight container in the refrigerator until ready to use.

A perfect combination — not only for vegetarians!

smashed pea, mint and Parmesan on crostini

½ loaf ciabatta or baguette, sliced into 20 x 8 mm slices

80 ml extra virgin olive oil

2 cups baby peas, blanched

½ clove garlic, peeled and roughly chopped

2 tbsp ground Parmesan

¼ cup parsley leaves, roughly chopped

2 tbsp mint leaves, roughly chopped

salt and pepper

makes 20 canapés

Preheat oven to 180°C. To make crostini, place bread slices on an oven tray and drizzle with half the olive oil. Bake for 3–4 minutes until the edges begin to turn golden brown. Remove from oven and allow to cool. Place peas, garlic and Parmesan in a food processor and pulse to a rough paste. Add remaining olive oil and herbs and mix to combine. Season to taste with a little salt and pepper. Spoon onto crostini and serve immediately.

dinner

Dinner is the main event and a chance to take the time to enjoy great food in the company of family and friends. From comfort food to elegant feasts, the dinner table should be the heart of every home.

Shockingly green and just as delicious!

green pea and ham soup

1 ham hock

1 onion, peeled and halved

1 stalk celery, roughly chopped

1 carrot, peeled and roughly chopped

3 cloves garlic, peeled

3 sprigs thyme

1 bay leaf

2½ litres water

300 g frozen baby peas

3 cups spinach, stalks removed

2 cups parsley leaves, washed

1 cup mint leaves, washed

salt and pepper

¼ cup crème fraîche

50 ml extra virgin olive oil

serves 4

Place ham hock in a medium-sized pot with onion, celery, carrot, garlic, thyme, bay leaf and water. Bring to a simmer over a medium to high heat, then reduce temperature and continue to simmer for 2 hours or until ham falls away from the bone. Remove from heat and strain off liquid. Reserve liquid in a large bowl and skim off any fat that may rise to the surface. Allow ham hock to cool before picking meat from bone and reserving for later use.

Place ham stock in a small pot and bring back to a simmer over a medium heat. In a separate large pot of lightly salted boiling water, blanch baby peas for 1 minute before straining in a large colander and refreshing under cold running water until peas are completely cool. In 2–3 batches place peas, spinach, parsley and mint with a little salt and pepper in a blender and process with just enough hot stock to allow the mixture to move in the blender. Blend until as smooth as possible before pouring out onto a flat oven tray or roasting dish and cooling in the refrigerator to retain the bright green colour.

When ready to serve, heat pea purée in a medium-sized heavy-based pot over a medium heat with half the remaining ham stock. Bring to the boil and adjust the consistency as desired with a little more stock, seasoning to taste with a little salt and pepper, if required. Place half the shredded ham in the bottom of four soup bowls, ladle hot pea soup over the top and finish with remaining ham, a spoon of crème fraîche, a sprinkle of pepper and a drizzle of olive oil. Serve immediately.

I love celeriac and this soup allows the subtle flavour of this amazing vegetable to shine through.

celeriac soup with hot-smoked salmon and crème fraîche

1 kg celeriac, peeled and cut into 2 cm cubes

1 litre milk

300 ml cream

salt and pepper

150 g hot-smoked salmon (see page 203)

100 g crème fraîche

2 tbsp finely chopped chives

extra virgin olive oil, to serve

1 loaf ciabatta, sliced and toasted

serves 4

Place celeriac in a heavy-based pot and cover with milk. Place a piece of baking paper over the milk in the pot to create a paper lid or cartouche (see page 205). Bring to the boil over a low to medium heat, reduce heat slightly and simmer for 25–30 minutes or until tender. Strain celeriac and reserve liquor.

Meanwhile, bring the cream to the boil in another pot. Place celeriac in a food processor and blend until smooth. Add boiled cream and half the reserved cooking liquor and blend to combine. Add a little more cooking liquor if a thinner consistency is desired. Season to taste with a little salt and pepper.

Divide soup between four bowls and finish with hot-smoked salmon, crème fraîche, a sprinkle of pepper and chives. Serve with a drizzle of extra virgin olive oil and toasted ciabatta.

Baby beetroot is one of the garden's absolute treats. Freshly dug and roasted, it is unbelievably sweet, and teamed with goat's curd and rocket it makes for a perfect salad. Boiled, it lends itself well to red meat and game, and the young leaves, quickly blanched and finished with a splash of olive oil, are delicious.

Baby beetroot is at its best when it reaches roughly golf ball size and is surprisingly tender and quick to cook. And, finally, as a solution to nasty artificial colours, beetroot can be juiced and used in small amounts as a natural red food colouring. Perfect for the next kids' party!

Vibrant in colour, this soup tastes as good as it looks.

beetroot soup with hung yoghurt and chives

8 large beetroot, peeled

salt and pepper

½ cup hung yoghurt
(see below)

¼ cup chives, finely chopped

30 ml extra virgin olive oil

serves 4

Place 4 beetroot in a medium-sized pot, cover with water and bring to the boil over a high heat. Reduce heat and simmer for 30 minutes or until beetroot are cooked and tender. Allow to cool in the cooking liquor, then grate. Juice remaining 4 beetroot through an electric juicer, then place juice in a medium-sized pot with grated, cooked beetroot. Bring liquid to the boil over a high heat, reduce heat and simmer for 10–15 minutes before removing from heat and passing through a fine sieve. Return liquid to a clean pot, bring to the boil once again, season to taste with a little salt and pepper and divide between four bowls. Place a spoonful of hung yoghurt in the centre of each bowl and top with chives. Drizzle with olive oil and serve immediately.

hung yoghurt

1 cup natural yoghurt

makes ½ cup

Place yoghurt in a square of muslin and tie with string to secure ends. Hang muslin overnight in the refrigerator over a bowl to contain liquid that will drain from the yoghurt. Remove yoghurt from muslin the following day, discard drained liquid and store hung yoghurt in an airtight container until ready to use or for up to one week.

Taste and texture combined, this hearty soup is sure to satisfy.

tomato, chickpea and saffron soup

50 ml olive oil

1 brown onion, peeled and roughly chopped

1 head fennel, outer layer removed and roughly chopped

1 medium carrot, peeled and roughly chopped

1 stalk celery, roughly chopped

1 head garlic, peeled and finely sliced

2 pinches dried chilli flakes

¼ tsp saffron

2 x 400 g cans chopped Italian tomatoes

1½ cups chickpeas, cooked and drained

300 ml chicken or vegetable stock

2 tsp caster sugar

¼ cup parsley leaves, finely chopped

salt and pepper

extra virgin olive oil

serves 4

Heat olive oil in a medium-sized heavy-based pot over a medium heat. Add onion, fennel, carrot and celery and sweat without colouring for 10 minutes. Add garlic and chilli flakes and continue to sweat for a further 2 minutes before adding saffron, tomatoes and chickpeas. Bring to the boil, reduce heat and simmer for 15–20 minutes. Add stock and sugar and cook for a further 5 minutes before stirring in parsley and seasoning to taste with a little salt and pepper. Divide between four bowls and drizzle with extra virgin olive oil. Serve immediately.

prawn, chilli, coconut and pumpkin soup

20 green prawns

100 ml peanut oil

1 small brown onion, peeled and roughly chopped

1 medium carrot, peeled and roughly chopped

1 small stalk celery, roughly chopped

16 cloves garlic, peeled

1 tsp tomato paste

1 x 5 cm knob fresh ginger, peeled and cut into fine strips

3 red chillies, seeds removed and finely sliced

1 medium butternut pumpkin, peeled, seeds removed and cut into 3 cm pieces

1 medium potato, peeled and cut into 3 cm pieces

2 tsp ground turmeric

1 tsp ground ginger

1 x 400 ml can good-quality coconut cream

2 tbsp fish sauce

juice of 2 limes

zest of 1 lime

salt and pepper

2 cups green beans, finely sliced

½ cup coriander leaves, washed

1 spring onion, finely sliced

serves 4

Peel and devein prawns and place in refrigerator for later use. In a separate container, reserve shells and heads. Heat 30 ml peanut oil in a medium-sized heavy-based pot over a medium heat. Add onion, carrot, celery and half the garlic and sweat for 5 minutes without colouring. Add prawn shells and heads to the pot and sweat for 3-4 minutes before adding tomato paste and cooking for a further minute. Add 1 litre water and bring to the boil. Reduce temperature and simmer for 20 minutes, skimming off any scum that rises to the surface. Strain and reserve prawn stock for later use.

Heat remaining peanut oil in a medium-sized saucepan over a medium to low heat. Finely slice remaining garlic and sweat with ginger and two-thirds of the chopped chilli, without colouring for 3 minutes. Add pumpkin and potato and cook for a further 2-3 minutes before adding dry spices. Cook for 1 minute before adding prawn stock and coconut cream. Bring to the boil then reduce temperature and simmer until pumpkin and potato are tender and just starting to break down. Add fish sauce, lime juice and zest and adjust seasoning with salt and pepper to taste. Roughly chop the peeled prawns and add with the beans to the soup. Simmer for a further minute then divide between four bowls. Finish with coriander, spring onion and remaining sliced chilli. Serve immediately.

gazpacho with paddle crab

4 live paddle crabs

4 large ripe red tomatoes

4 red capsicums, cores and seeds removed

1 small telegraph cucumber

½ small red onion, peeled

1 clove garlic, peeled

100 ml extra virgin olive oil

75 ml good-quality red wine vinegar

sea salt

freshly ground black pepper

¼ cup chives, finely chopped

serves 4

Place paddle crabs in the freezer for 1 hour to prepare humanely. Remove from freezer and place in a large pot of salted boiling water. Once water comes back to the boil, cook crabs for a further 4 minutes then remove from the pot, using a slotted spoon, and plunge into iced water to cool completely. Once cool, remove, from iced water and drain. Remove the top shell and the dead man's fingers (gills), and pick crab meat using a lobster picker or bamboo skewer. Refrigerate crab meat until ready to use.

To make gazpacho, roughly chop vegetables and blend in a food processor on high speed until as smooth as possible. Pass through a coarse sieve or mouli, add olive oil and vinegar, mix well and season to taste with salt and pepper. Place gazpacho in a stainless steel bowl and chill completely, either in a refrigerator or over ice. Once chilled, divide between four bowls, scatter with freshly picked paddle crab and chives, and serve immediately.

It's hard to imagine cooking without garlic, so it goes without saying that garlic is an important crop in any good garden. Imported garlic can often be of poor quality and the locally grown stuff can prove costly if you like to use a fair bit, so the solution is to grow your own and reap the rewards.

The time-old advice of planting on the shortest day and harvesting on the longest still holds true but, in fact, you can bend these rules a little on either side to stretch the crop and have new season garlic available for longer. The most important rule is to plant healthy, disease-free garlic cloves as this will govern the state of the garlic when it is harvested. There are many varieties available but, lucky for us, local Kakanui garlic is still one of the best!

Del, the charming Englishman in our kitchen, loves a good lamb's fry. And judging by how popular it is in the restaurant, he's definitely not alone.

lamb's fry with bacon, garlic mash and onion gravy

6 fresh lamb kidneys

1 fresh lamb liver

1 recipe mashed potato (see page 196)

2 heads confit garlic (see page 202)
or 1 clove raw garlic, peeled and crushed

50 ml olive oil

salt and pepper

16 slices streaky bacon, grilled until crisp

2 cups onion gravy (recipe follows)

serves 4

Preheat oven to 180°C. Prepare offal by removing outer membranes. Slice kidneys in half lengthwise, trim and remove white ducting with scissors or a sharp knife. Cut liver into long, thin slices, discarding any blood vessels.

Heat mash in a small pot over a medium heat. Add confit garlic to mashed potatoes and mix well to combine.

Heat olive oil in a large heavy-based frying pan over a high heat. Season offal with a little salt and pepper. Fry kidneys for 1 minute on each side and fry liver for 30 seconds on each side. Remove from pan and keep warm. Place bacon in oven to reheat.

To serve, place lamb's fry over garlic mash, spoon onion gravy over the top and finish with bacon.

onion gravy

6 medium brown onions, peeled and finely sliced

50 ml olive oil

1 tbsp unsalted butter

1 cup jus (see page 204)

1 tbsp red wine vinegar

1 tsp thyme leaves, finely chopped

makes 2 cups

Place onions in a medium-sized saucepan with olive oil and butter over a medium heat. Cook without colouring until onions are very soft and almost of jam consistency. Add jus and bring to the boil. Remove from heat, add vinegar and thyme and allow to cool before storing in the refrigerator until ready to use.

A favourite with both customers and staff every time we put it on!

duck and wild mushroom pappardelle

1½ cups dried wild mushrooms

1 x size 22 duck, trimmed, with excess fat removed

100 ml olive oil

salt and pepper

1 tbsp unsalted butter

½ medium carrot, peeled and finely diced

1 small brown onion, peeled and finely diced

½ stalk celery, finely diced

5 cloves garlic, peeled and finely sliced

1 bay leaf

¼ cup sage leaves, finely chopped

1 tbsp tomato paste

350 ml red wine

1 cup water

1 recipe fresh pappardelle
(see page 194)

½ cup parsley leaves, finely chopped

¼ cup ground Parmesan

serves 4

Preheat oven to 190°C. Place dried wild mushrooms in a small bowl and cover with warm water for at least 30 minutes to soften. Place duck, breast-side up, in a roasting pan and brush with a little of the olive oil. Season duck skin and the inside of the duck cavity with a little salt and pepper. Smear the top of the duck with butter and roast for 40 minutes before reducing temperature to 150°C and roasting for a further 2 hours or until duck is tender. Remove duck from oven and allow to cool before removing meat from the carcass and reserving for later use.

Heat remaining olive oil in a medium-sized heavy-based pot over a medium heat and sweat carrot, onion, celery and garlic, without colouring, for 15 minutes. Remove mushrooms from the soaking liquor (saving mushroom stock) and roughly chop. Add mushrooms to vegetables and cook for a further 5 minutes before adding bay leaf, sage and tomato paste. Cook out the tomato paste for 2 minutes, add mushroom stock and reduce until liquid has almost disappeared. Add red wine and reduce by half before adding the water and the roasted duck meat. Bring to the boil, adjust seasoning with a little salt and pepper, reduce heat and simmer duck and mushroom sauce for 15 minutes before removing from heat. Keep warm until ready to use. Adjust consistency with a little more water if the sauce is too thick, or simmer a little longer to thicken as required.

Bring a large pot of lightly salted water to the boil. Place pappardelle into boiling water and cook for 1 minute after water returns to the boil. Once pasta is cooked, drain well in a colander and toss in a large bowl with duck and mushroom sauce to combine. Divide between four large plates, finish with parsley and Parmesan and serve immediately.

Florence fennel. Right at the top of my list, it always seems we can never grow enough of it! A tender, young fennel bulb can be shaved fresh into salads, adding a delightful crunch and a subtle aniseed flavour, or roasted as a divine accompaniment to fish, lamb or pork. The feathery tops can also be picked for salads, sauces and marinades. Easily grown in autumn and spring, fennel is a welcome addition to any cook's garden.

Completely underrated, flounder, like all flatfish, has moist, sweet flesh that is absolutely delicious.

whole pan-fried flounder with capers, burnt butter and lemon

1 cup plain flour

1 tsp salt

½ tsp freshly ground black pepper

2 whole (350–400 g) flounder, scaled and gutted

60 ml olive oil

100 g unsalted butter

4 tbsp baby capers, rinsed

juice of ½ lemon

4 tbsp parsley leaves, finely chopped

2 cups salad greens

½ fennel bulb, finely sliced

½ lemon, quartered

serves 2

Preheat oven to 200°C. Place flour in a large bowl with salt and pepper and mix to combine. Dust flounder on both sides in the seasoned flour. Heat olive oil in two large heavy-based ovenproof frying pans over a high heat. Place fish, top-side down, into pans and fry for 2 minutes before adding a knob of butter to each pan and placing in the oven. Roast for 5 minutes before turning each fish over and cooking for a further 3 minutes. Carefully remove from oven and allow to rest in the pans for 2 minutes.

Transfer to two warm plates. Return one of the pans back to a high heat, add remaining butter and cook until it starts to turn dark brown. Add capers and fry until crisp and butter begins to burn. Remove from heat and add lemon juice and parsley. Spoon burnt butter, capers and parsley over fish and serve with salad greens, fennel and a wedge of lemon.

Rich and sticky, this is winter goodness at its best.

slow-cooked lamb with potato gnocchi and parsley oil

1 kg lamb shoulder, bone in

1 x 400 g can chopped Italian tomatoes

2 cups water

200 ml jus, warmed (see page 204)

150 ml olive oil

24 pieces potato gnocchi (see page 195)

½ cup parsley leaves, washed

½ tsp salt

serves 4

Preheat oven to 200°C. Place lamb in a large roasting dish with tomatoes and the water. Cover and seal tightly with aluminium foil. Place in oven and cook for 30 minutes before reducing temperature to 150°C and continuing to roast for 2–3 hours or until lamb is extremely tender and falling from the bone. Remove lamb from oven and allow to cool before picking meat from the shoulder and discarding any bones and fat. Increase oven temperature to 200°C. Place lamb in a large heavy-based frying pan with jus and return to oven, basting occasionally with jus.

Heat 50 ml olive oil in a large non-stick frying pan over a medium to high heat. Add gnocchi and colour one side until golden brown. Turn gnocchi over in the pan and place in the oven for 4–5 minutes.

To make parsley oil, place parsley and salt in a mortar and grind to a smooth paste. Add remaining olive oil and muddle together.

Remove gnocchi from oven and divide between four plates. Top with lamb and reduced jus juices. Finish with a drizzle of parsley oil and serve immediately.

Prosciutto, sage and lemon make a magical combination that works particularly well with veal.

veal saltimbocca with sautéed potatoes and roast asparagus

2 x 150 g pieces veal tenderloin

8 slices thin prosciutto

30 sage leaves

120 ml olive oil

4 small Agria potatoes, boiled and sliced into rounds

salt

12 spears asparagus

30 g unsalted butter

juice of ½ lemon

40 ml Marsala or Bristol Cream sherry

jus, warmed, to serve (see page 204)

serves 2

Preheat oven to 180°C. Cut veal pieces into four. Flatten each piece with a meat mallet to 5 mm thick. Lay prosciutto slices on a clean, flat surface and place two sage leaves on top of each slice. Place veal over one end of the prosciutto and gently wrap to form a flat parcel.

Heat one-third of the olive oil in a large heavy-based ovenproof frying pan over a high heat. Add potatoes, season with a little salt and fry until golden on both sides. Remove from pan and reserve in a warm place. Clean pan using absorbent kitchen paper, then heat half the remaining olive oil over a high heat. Add asparagus to pan and colour on one side before turning over and roasting in the oven for 3–4 minutes. Remove asparagus from oven and keep warm.

In a separate large heavy-based frying pan, heat remaining olive oil over a high heat and quickly fry veal until crisp and coloured on both sides. Remove from pan and rest in a warm place. Add butter to pan and brown over a high heat until butter begins to burn. Add remaining sage leaves, cook for 5 seconds, remove pan from heat and immediately add lemon juice and Marsala or sherry.

Divide potatoes, asparagus and veal between two plates and spoon burnt butter and sage sauce over the top. Serve with a splash of jus and a wedge of lemon, if desired.

Comfort can always be found at the end of a lamb chop!

lamb cutlets with hummus, parsley and red onion salad

2 lamb racks, trimmed

salt and pepper

30 ml olive oil

1½ cups hummus (see page 198)

2 cups parsley leaves, washed

1 medium red onion, finely sliced

50 ml extra virgin olive oil

juice of 1 lemon

serves 4

Preheat oven to 200°C. Score silverskin or thin layer of fat on the top of lamb racks and lightly season with salt and pepper. Heat olive oil in a large heavy-based frying pan over a medium to high heat and seal lamb racks on all sides until golden brown. Turn racks over in pan, scored-side down, and roast in oven for 10–12 minutes or until medium-rare. Remove lamb from oven and allow to rest in pan for at least 7–8 minutes.

Spread hummus on four plates. Carve lamb into cutlets and place over hummus. Scatter a little parsley and red onion over lamb and drizzle with extra virgin olive oil. Toss remaining parsley and red onion together in a bowl, dress with extra virgin olive oil and lemon juice and serve on the side.

New Zealand has some of the best salmon in the world. Teamed with avocado salsa, it's a match made in heaven.

seared salmon with avocado salsa

150 ml olive oil

juice and zest of 1 lime

2 tbsp mango or apricot chutney

½ tsp ground cumin

2 cups coriander leaves, roughly chopped

1 long red chilli, seeds removed and finely chopped

¼ small red onion, finely chopped

2 large ripe avocados, peeled, pit removed and cubed

salt and pepper

4 x 180 g salmon fillets, skin on and pin-boned

2 cups baby rocket

2 limes, halved

serves 4

To make salsa, place 100 ml olive oil, lime juice and zest, chutney, cumin, coriander, chilli and onion in a large bowl. Add avocado and gently mix together. Season salsa to taste with a little salt and pepper and refrigerate for further use.

Season salmon fillets with salt and pepper on both sides. Heat remaining olive oil in a large heavy-based frying pan over a high heat. When oil starts to smoke add salmon fillets and fry, skin-side down, for 3 minutes. When salmon is two-thirds cooked, turn and cook for a further minute before removing from the pan and allowing to rest in a warm place.

Divide avocado salsa between four plates, top with baby rocket and finish with salmon on top. Serve immediately with half a lime.

If food is all about flavour, then this dish is what it's all about!

slow-roast Asian pork with salad of cucumber, chilli and soy

1 kg fresh pork shoulder, bone removed

1 tsp salt

1 pinch dried chilli flakes

2 tsp coriander seeds, roasted and ground

4 cloves garlic, peeled and roughly chopped

1 x 5 cm knob fresh ginger, peeled and roughly chopped

2 tbsp vegetable oil

½ cup water

½ telegraph cucumber, finely sliced lengthways, using a potato peeler

2 cups coriander leaves, washed

2 red chillies, seeds removed and finely sliced

½ cup mint leaves, washed

1 cup finely sliced spring onions

1 cup baby spinach leaves

1 cup basil leaves, washed (optional)

½ cup Vietnamese mint leaves, washed (optional)

3 cups cooked jasmine rice

¾ cup soy, chilli and garlic dressing (see page 200)

serves 4

Preheat oven to 200°C. To prepare pork, score skin with a very sharp knife. Crush salt, chilli flakes and coriander seeds in a mortar. Add garlic and ginger and grind to a smooth paste. Muddle with vegetable oil and smear spice mix all over the skin and the flesh of the pork. Place in a roasting dish with 6–10 cm sides and cook for 30 minutes. Remove pork, add the water to the roasting dish and cover with aluminium foil. Reduce oven to 150°C before returning pork to oven and cooking for a further 2½ hours or until meat is falling apart. Remove from oven and allow to rest for at least 15 minutes before serving.

In a stainless steel bowl, gently toss salad ingredients together and reserve. Gently heat jasmine rice and divide between four plates. Remove skin and excess fat from pork, portion and serve on top of rice. Drizzle generously with soy, chilli and garlic dressing and top with salad greens. Serve immediately with a little extra dressing, if desired.

Baby carrots represent what having your own garden is all about. Small in size yet big on taste they are so easy to grow, and all that is required is a small space of well-composted soil, regular watering and a little sunshine. Sow seeds in thin, evenly spaced rows and harvest after 7–8 weeks when carrots are about the size of your fingers. Baby carrots require no peeling and take only seconds to cook. They go well with just about anything boiled, roasted or raw — and pulled straight from the garden, wiped off and eaten, they are the stuff memories are made of!

A dish I learnt to make in London and one I still use today.

seared white fish with champ, baby peas and bacon

100 g streaky bacon, cut into small batons

80 ml olive oil

3 cloves garlic, peeled and finely sliced

2 cups cream

salt and pepper

16 baby carrots

2 cups baby peas

1 recipe mashed potato (see page 196)

2 tbsp parsley leaves, finely chopped

800 g white fish fillets (gurnard, tarakihi, snapper or brill)

5 spring onions, finely sliced

serves 4

Place bacon and 1 tbsp olive oil in a small pot and cook over a medium heat until bacon is crisp. Add garlic and sweat for 30 seconds before adding cream and bringing to the boil. Reduce temperature and simmer for 2 minutes before removing sauce from heat and adjusting seasoning with a little salt and pepper. Reserve for later use.

Blanch carrots in a medium-sized pot of lightly salted boiling water until tender. Remove carrots with a slotted spoon and refresh with cold running water. Blanch baby peas in the same pot then drain and refresh, reserving both for later use. Warm mashed potato in a small pot over a medium heat. Stir often with a wooden spoon to prevent potatoes from catching on the bottom. Meanwhile, bring cream sauce back to the boil, add peas and carrots and continue to heat until sauce returns to the boil. Remove from heat, add parsley and keep warm.

Heat half the remaining olive oil in a large non-stick frying pan over a high heat. Cook fish fillets, in batches, for 2 minutes on each side or until just cooked. Mix spring onions into mashed potato and place a spoonful of champ into four bowls. Ladle peas, carrots, bacon and sauce next to champ before placing fish fillets on top and serving immediately.

Pomegranate molasses goes beautifully with most game, particularly venison.

seared venison with roast vegetables and pomegranate molasses

8 baby beetroot, stalks removed

6 baby turnips, stalks removed

12 baby carrots, leaves removed

120 ml olive oil

salt and pepper

½ cup water

600 g Denver leg venison, cut into 4 pieces

80 ml pomegranate molasses

1 bunch ruby chard, stems removed

½ cup pomegranate seeds (optional)

serves 4

Preheat oven to 180°C. Place beetroot, turnips and carrots in a baking paper-lined roasting tray. Drizzle with 80 ml olive oil and season with salt and pepper. Pour the water into tray, cover and seal sides with aluminium foil. Roast for 30–40 minutes or until tender. When cooked, remove from oven and allow to cool completely before removing aluminium foil.

Lightly season venison with a little salt and pepper and place in a small bowl. Add half the pomegranate molasses, coating venison on all sides. Heat remaining olive oil in a large heavy-based frying pan over a high heat. Sear venison for 1 minute on all sides. Remove venison from pan and allow to rest in a warm place for at least 5 minutes.

Place vegetables back in oven for 5 minutes to reheat. Blanch chard for 1 minute in a small pot of boiling water. Remove from pot and drain. Return a clean frying pan to a high heat and quickly warm venison for 30 seconds on each side before removing from pan and carving. Remove vegetables from oven and divide between four plates. Top with chard and venison and finish with a drizzle of remaining pomegranate molasses and fresh pomegranate seeds, if desired. Serve immediately.

Accidents happen all the time in the countryside so, should a pheasant happen to crease the bonnet of your car, make the most of an unfortunate situation with a lovely dinner for two. Easier to take home than a deer!

roast pheasant with puy lentils, red wine onions and baby carrots

2 large brown onions, skin on, ends trimmed, cut into 1 cm-thick rings

80 ml olive oil

¼ cup soft brown sugar

1 cup red wine

10 baby carrots

1 pheasant, plucked, gutted and hung for 3–4 days

salt and pepper

1 cup puy lentils, boiled until tender, then drained

100 ml jus (see page 204)

1 tbsp parsley leaves, finely chopped

1 cup baby spinach

serves 2

Preheat oven to 180°C. Place onion rings in a baking paper-lined roasting tray and drizzle with half the olive oil. Sprinkle with sugar and douse with red wine. Cover and seal tray with aluminium foil and roast for 30 minutes or until onions are tender. Remove aluminium foil from tray and roast a further 5 minutes before removing onions from oven and allowing to cool.

Place carrots in a separate baking paper-lined roasting tray and drizzle with half the remaining olive oil and ½ cup water. Cover with aluminium foil and roast for 25 minutes until carrots are tender. Remove from oven and keep warm.

Trim neck, feet and wings from pheasant and discard. Heat remaining olive oil in a large heavy-based ovenproof frying pan over a medium heat. Season pheasant with a little salt and pepper and sear on all sides. Turn pheasant, breast-side up, in the pan and roast in over for 30 minutes. Remove from oven and allow to rest in the pan in a warm place.

Remove tough outer layers of onion skin and warm with the lentils in a small saucepan with half the jus. Stir in parsley and divide between two plates. Plate carrots and spinach on top. Carve and serve pheasant and finish with remaining jus.

An unusual vegetable at first sight, kohlrabi certainly is an eye-catcher! With its myriad shoots sprouting out of a swollen stem, kohlrabi is similar to a turnip and has a delicate, earthy flavour. Best eaten young, it can be shaved raw into salads, added to stir-fries, slow-roasted or cooked down to an elegant soup. Kohlrabi is a relatively easy vegetable to grow and keeps well once harvested, making it an ideal crop to help get you through the long, cold days of winter.

Roast kohlrabi makes a welcome change from potatoes and, combined with fresh horseradish, goes particularly well with beef.

rib-eye of beef with roast kohlrabi and horseradish

150 ml olive oil

800 g kohlrabi, peeled and cut into 2 cm pieces

2 tbsp unsalted butter

6 cloves garlic, peeled and finely sliced

salt and pepper

½ cup water

4 x 250 g rib-eye steaks

4 tbsp grated fresh horseradish

2 tbsp crème fraîche

1 cup parsley leaves, roughly chopped

1½ tbsp lemon juice

1 bunch ruby chard, stalks removed

120 ml jus, optional (see page 204)

serves 4

Preheat oven to 180°C. Heat 100 ml olive oil in an ovenproof frying pan over a medium heat. Add kohlrabi and butter and sauté until kohlrabi begins to colour. Add garlic, lightly season with salt and pepper and place with the water in a baking paper-lined roasting tray. Cover tray with aluminium foil, making sure you seal all edges, and roast for 30–40 minutes or until tender. Remove from oven and reserve in a warm place until ready to serve.

Heat remaining olive oil in a large heavy-based frying pan over a high heat until oil just begins to smoke. Season steaks with a little salt and pepper on both sides and cook for 4–5 minutes or until a good colour is achieved. Turn steaks over and cook for a further 3 minutes. Remove steaks from pan and rest for at least 5 minutes in a warm place.

Return kohlrabi to oven for 2 minutes to bring it back up to temperature. Remove from oven and place kohlrabi in a bowl with horseradish, crème fraîche, parsley and lemon juice. Mix together well, season to taste with a little salt and pepper and divide between four plates. Blanch ruby chard for 30–40 seconds in a large pot of boiling, salted water. Drain and place on top of kohlrabi. Place steaks on top of greens and finish with a little jus, if desired. Serve immediately.

sides

Never underestimate a good
side dish. Paired well with a main,
it can make a good meal great!

Sometimes it's easy to forget how delicious simple food can be.

tomato and basil salad

500 g mixed heirloom tomatoes,
washed

30 ml extra virgin olive oil

2 tsp balsamic vinegar

salt and pepper

¼ small red onion, finely sliced

¼ cup basil leaves, washed

serves 2 as a side

Slice small tomatoes in half and any larger varieties into thick slices, according to size. Place tomatoes in a serving bowl and drizzle with extra virgin olive oil and balsamic vinegar. Season lightly with salt and pepper and scatter with sliced onions and basil before serving.

One of the most striking vegetables you can grow, Romanesco broccoli, with its tightly spiralling minarets, is a marvel to behold both in the garden and on the plate. Growing similarly to a cauliflower, Romanesco's florets form, almost hidden away, beneath a swath of closely knit outer leaves until, at last, they finally reveal themselves in all their glory.

Slicing and blanching is all that is required to cook Romanesco broccoli, but it can also be slow-cooked in olive oil until it starts to break down then added to anchovies, garlic, chilli and olives to make a delicious Italian sauce. Like common broccoli, Romanesco prefers the cooler months of spring and autumn, so plan when planting to make the most of this handsome Italian!

An ideal way to show off this striking vegetable.

Romanesco broccoli with agrodolce

1 large head Romanesco broccoli
salt and pepper
1½ cups agrodolce, at room temperature (see below)

serves 4 as a side

Place a large heavy-based pot of lightly salted water over a high heat and bring to the boil. Cut broccoli into florets and blanch for 1 minute. Remove with a slotted spoon and place in a serving bowl. Lightly season broccoli with salt and pepper and serve with agrodolce spooned over the top to finish.

agrodolce

½ cup currants
½ cup red wine vinegar
½ clove garlic, peeled
½ tsp salt
½ cup extra virgin olive oil
1 tsp soft brown sugar
½ cup pine nuts, lightly roasted
¼ cup parsley leaves, finely chopped

makes 1½ cups

Soak currants in red wine vinegar in a small bowl overnight. Place garlic and salt in a mortar and grind to a smooth paste. Warm half the olive oil in a small saucepan over a medium heat. Add crushed garlic and cook for 20 seconds, without colouring, before adding sugar, currants and vinegar. Cook for a further 2 minutes before removing from the heat and allowing to cool. Add pine nuts, parsley and remaining olive oil and mix to combine.

Store in an airtight container in the refrigerator for up to five days.

For an explosion of colour, edible flowers are the perfect way to impress.

edible flower salad

1 tbsp chardonnay vinegar

1 tbsp extra virgin olive oil

¼ tsp caster sugar

16 nasturtium flowers

12 runner bean flowers

12 rocket flowers

12 snow pea flowers

12 violas

2 heads chive flowers, petals picked

5 calendula flowers, petals picked

3 edible roses, petals picked

3 hemerocallis daylilies, petals picked

serves 4 as a side

Whisk vinegar, olive oil and sugar together in a small bowl and drizzle onto a large serving plate. Scatter flowers over dressing and serve immediately.

IMPORTANT!
Check with a reliable source before picking and eating any flowers. Not all flowers are edible so caution must be exercised. If there is any doubt, it's best not to eat them.

Beetroot and goat's curd are perfect partners, and I never tire of this combination.

roast baby beetroot with goat's curd

600 g baby beetroot

80 ml olive oil

salt and pepper

5–6 sprigs fresh thyme

1 head garlic, cut in half crossways

½ cup water or chicken stock
(see page 205)

100 g fresh goat's curd

30 ml extra virgin olive oil

serves 2 as a side

Preheat oven to 180°C. If beetroot are bigger than a golf ball, slice in half lengthways through the stem, running down to the tip. Place beetroot on a small baking paper-lined oven tray, drizzle with 50 ml olive oil and season with a little salt and pepper. Scatter thyme and garlic over beetroot before adding water or stock to the tray. Cover and seal sides with aluminium foil and roast for 30–40 minutes or until tender. To test beetroot, simply skewer with a small, sharp knife. When cooked, remove beetroot from oven and allow to cool completely before removing aluminium foil. Remove skin by simply rubbing off with your fingers or using a sharp knife.

When ready to serve, place beetroot on a baking paper-lined oven tray and drizzle with remaining olive oil and a little salt and pepper. Place in oven for 5 minutes to reheat before transferring to a serving bowl. Crumble goat's curd over beetroot and finish with a drizzle of extra virgin olive oil.

This sauce is absolutely divine and is fabulous with freshly picked green beans, straight from the garden.

green beans and romesco sauce

2 large ripe tomatoes, cut in half

1 red chilli, seeds removed

1 clove garlic, peeled

200 ml olive oil

1 red capsicum, roasted, skin and seeds removed

3 slices ciabatta

¼ cup hazelnuts, roasted, peeled and crushed

2 tbsp red wine vinegar

salt and pepper

350 g green beans, trimmed

serves 4 as a side

Preheat oven to 180°C. To make romesco sauce, place tomatoes, chilli and garlic on a baking paper-lined oven tray and drizzle with 50 ml olive oil. Roast for 10–15 minutes until vegetables are soft and just starting to colour. Remove from oven and place in a food processor with roasted capsicum. Blend until smooth. Lightly toast ciabatta, add half to the vegetables and pulse to combine. Place sauce in a small stainless steel bowl, then mix in hazelnuts, remaining olive oil and red wine vinegar. Season to taste with a little salt and pepper, and set aside.

Bring a medium-sized pot of water to the boil over a high heat. Add beans and blanch for 40–50 seconds. Remove beans from pot, drain and place in a serving bowl. Roughly tear remaining toasted ciabatta and scatter over beans before topping with romesco sauce and serving immediately.

Everyone's favourite in the restaurant, this dish has changed the way we think about cabbage.

shaved cabbage salad with roast hazelnuts, Parmesan and balsamic

3 cups very finely sliced drumhead cabbage

¼ small red onion, finely sliced

2 spring onions, finely chopped

½ tsp wholegrain mustard

juice of ¼ lemon

30 ml olive oil

2 tbsp aged balsamic vinegar

¼ cup whole hazelnuts, roasted and skins removed

2 tbsp ground Parmesan

extra virgin olive oil, to finish

serves 2 as a side

Place cabbage, red onion, spring onion, mustard and lemon juice in a large bowl. Drizzle with olive oil and lightly toss together. Place in a serving bowl before drizzling with balsamic vinegar. Top with hazelnuts and finish with Parmesan and a little extra virgin olive oil, if desired. Serve immediately.

sweet

A sweet offering to complete the experience!

A beautiful way to end any meal.

vanilla panna cotta with raspberry jelly and pistachio tuilles

1¾ gelatine leaves

75 ml cold milk

450 ml cream

60 g caster sugar

zest of ½ lemon

½ vanilla bean, cut lengthways and seeds scraped

200 ml raspberry jelly (see below)

6 pistachio tuilles (see page 206)

makes 6

Break gelatine leaves into thirds and place in a small bowl with milk to soften. Place half the cream in a small saucepan with the sugar, lemon zest and vanilla bean and seeds. Bring to a simmer over a medium heat before pouring onto milk and softened gelatine. Remove vanilla bean and stir until gelatine is completely dissolved. Half fill a large bowl with ice and chill the bowl containing panna cotta mixture on top. Stir often with a wooden spoon to prevent gelatine setting on the bottom of the bowl as it cools.

In a separate bowl, whisk remaining cream to soft peaks. When panna cotta mixture starts to thicken, gently fold in the cream. Pour into six 150 ml glasses, leaving a 2 cm gap from the top, and refrigerate until set. Warm jelly slightly and pour onto panna cottas. Refrigerate until jelly is set. Serve with pistachio tuilles.

raspberry jelly

400 g raspberries

80 g caster sugar

2½ gelatine leaves

makes 200 ml

Warm raspberries and caster sugar in a small pot over a medium heat, stirring occasionally, until juice begins to run from fruit. Remove from heat and pass through a fine sieve. Measure the total quantity of raspberry juice in a measuring jug. For every 100 ml of juice, break up 1 gelatine leaf into a small bowl and cover with cold water to soften. Once softened, remove gelatine from bowl, squeezing out any excess water. Place gelatine and raspberry juice in a small pot and warm until gelatine has dissolved completely. Refrigerate jelly until ready to use.

Few people can resist a good tarte Tatin!

pear tarte Tatin with salted caramel

1 x 20 cm x 20 cm puff pastry sheet
(see page 193)

4 ripe pears, peeled, quartered and
cores removed

1 cup salted caramel (see below)

vanilla bean ice cream, to serve
(see page 207)

serves 4

Preheat oven to 200°C. Cut four 10 cm rounds, 5 mm thick, from puff pastry sheet using a large cookie cutter. Dock pastry rounds with a fork to prevent pastry from over-rising. Place one-third of the caramel in the bottom of four 10 cm blini pans or round aluminium pie dishes placed on a baking tray. Place four pieces of pear, rounded sides down, into each pan with the caramel. Place pastry rounds on top of pears.

Bake in oven for 20–25 minutes or until pastry is crisp and golden brown. Remove from oven and allow to cool slightly before turning out onto four plates. Warm remaining caramel in a small pot over a low heat and drizzle over each tarte Tatin. Serve immediately with vanilla bean ice cream.

salted caramel

1½ cups caster sugar

½ cup water

½ cup unsalted butter, chopped

1 tsp salt

¼ cup cream

makes 2 cups

Place sugar and water in a medium-sized saucepan and bring to the boil over a high heat. Continue to boil until sugar begins to caramelize and starts to turn a deep golden brown. Add butter and whisk to combine, being careful to avoid resulting steam. Add salt and cream and continue to whisk over heat to combine. Remove from heat and allow to cool before storing in an airtight container in the refrigerator for up to two months.

Light, delicate and delectable.

rosewater meringues

4 large free-range egg whites

300 g caster sugar

2 tbsp rosewater

50 g cornflour

½ tsp fresh beetroot juice (or 2–3 drops pink food colouring)

½ cup rosewater syrup (see below)

1 cup cream, whipped

½ cup edible rose petals

serves 4

Preheat oven to 120°C. Line an oven tray with baking paper. Place egg whites in a large, clean, dry mixing bowl and whisk on medium to high speed until soft peaks are formed. Add sugar in three stages, whisking for 2 minutes between each addition. Reduce speed to low, add rosewater, cornflour and beetroot juice, then whisk for a further 30 seconds on high. Spoon meringue into small mounds on prepared oven tray and cook for 30 minutes before reducing temperature to 80°C and cooking for a further hour. Remove from oven and allow to cool completely before serving with rosewater syrup and fresh whipped cream and rose petals.

rosewater syrup

½ cup caster sugar

¼ cup water

1 tbsp rosewater

½ tsp fresh beetroot juice

makes ¾ cup

Place sugar and water in a small saucepan and bring to the boil over a medium to high heat. Continue to boil until sugar is dissolved and syrup is reduced by one-third. Remove from heat and allow to cool before stirring in rosewater and beetroot juice.

Store syrup in an airtight container in the refrigerator until ready to use.

This is my idea of a great dessert!

honeycomb and Drambuie ice cream sandwich with hazelnut praline

1 litre honeycomb ice cream
(see page 207)

75 ml Drambuie

16 ice cream wafers
(see below)

¼ cup vanilla Drambuie syrup
(see page 209)

½ cup hazelnut praline, lightly crushed
(see page 208)

icing sugar, to dust

serves 4

Place honeycomb ice cream and Drambuie in a large bowl, allow to soften slightly and mix together with a wooden spoon to combine. Line a terrine mould or small loaf tin with baking paper, fill with ice cream mix and freeze overnight. Remove ice cream from mould by running a little hot water over the back of the mould. Remove any baking paper from ice cream and slice into 1 cm slices. Place each ice cream slice between two wafers. Stack two ice cream wafer sandwiches on top of each other on four plates. Drizzle vanilla Drambuie syrup around each plate and finish with a sprinkle of hazelnut praline and a light dusting of icing sugar. Serve immediately.

ice cream wafers

60 g unsalted butter,
at room temperature

90 g soft brown sugar

2 tbsp golden syrup

1 large free-range egg

140 g plain flour

½ tsp baking soda

100 ml milk

makes 32 x 7 cm square wafers

Preheat oven to 180°C. Line two baking trays with baking paper. Place all ingredients in a mixing bowl and mix together until smooth. Using a steel crank-handled spatula, thinly and evenly spread wafer mix over the baking paper. Bake for 5–6 minutes or until golden brown. Remove from oven and cut into 7 cm x 7 cm squares while wafers are still hot. Allow to cool completely before storing in an airtight container for up to one week.

So simple, this is summer in a bowl.

summer berry salad with milk gelato

2 cups fresh cherries

1 cup fresh blackberries

2 cups fresh raspberries

1 cup fresh boysenberries

milk gelato (see below)

icing sugar, to dust (optional)

serves 4

Scatter fruit between four bowls and top with milk gelato. Dust with icing sugar, if desired, and serve immediately.

milk gelato

600 ml full cream milk

200 ml cream

50 g milk powder

150 g liquid glucose

70 g caster sugar

makes 1 litre

Place all ingredients in a heavy-based saucepan and stir over a medium to high heat until gelato base reaches 80°C (use a heatproof thermometer to test the temperature). Remove from heat, transfer to a stainless steel bowl and refrigerate until completely cold.

Churn in an ice-cream machine according to manufacturer's instructions.

Sometimes chocolate is just not enough!

drunken chocolate torte with vanilla rum syrup

330 g whole almonds, blanched

330 g dark chocolate

330 g caster sugar

1½ cups dark rum

330 g unsalted butter

9 free-range eggs, separated

vanilla rum syrup, to serve
(see below)

rum and raisin ice cream, to serve
(see page 206)

serves 12

Preheat oven to 160°C. Grease and line a round 28 cm cake tin with removable base with baking paper. Place almonds and chocolate in a food processor and blend until completely ground. Add sugar and continue to process for a further minute before adding the rum while the machine is still running. Continue to process until mixture forms a smooth paste. Leaving the machine on, add butter, processing to combine, before adding egg yolks, one at a time. Remove chocolate mixture from the food processor and place in a large mixing bowl. Whisk egg whites to a firm peak and fold into chocolate mixture. Pour into prepared cake tin and bake for 1¼ hours or until just set. Remove from oven and allow to cool completely before serving with a drizzle of vanilla rum syrup and some rum and raisin ice cream.

vanilla rum syrup

1 cup caster sugar

¾ cup water

½ tsp vanilla bean paste

1 tbsp dark rum

makes 1 cup

Place sugar, water and vanilla paste in a small saucepan and bring to the boil over a medium to high heat. Remove from heat and allow to cool completely. Stir in rum and store in an airtight container for up to one month.

As good as it looks, this tart is a real crowd-pleaser.

chocolate tart with fresh raspberries

650 g 70% dark chocolate buttons

350 ml milk

220 g unsalted butter, softened

250 g caster sugar

3 free-range egg yolks

1 recipe sweet short crust pastry, blind baked (see page 192)

800 g fresh raspberries

150 ml fresh cream, lightly whipped, to serve (optional)

serves 10

Place chocolate and milk in a stainless steel bowl. Heat over a large pot of simmering water, stirring until chocolate has melted. Cream butter and sugar until pale and creamy, add egg yolks and mix well. Stir the creamed mixture into the warm chocolate until well combined. Pour into cooked pastry case and refrigerate for 1½ hours.

Remove tart from tart tin and place gently on a flat serving plate. Scatter raspberries over tart. Slice with a very hot knife and serve with fresh cream, if desired.

Moist and delicious, this cake is also gluten-free. And the sorbet is to die for!

crushed pineapple and coconut cake with coconut and lime sorbet

350 g unsalted butter, softened

350 g caster sugar

8 free-range eggs

2½ tsp baking powder

280 g ground almonds

200 g desiccated coconut

coconut and lime sorbet, to serve (see below)

500 g crushed pineapple (unsweetened), plus extra to serve

serves 10

Preheat oven to 160°C. Lightly grease and line a 28 cm cake tin with removable base with baking paper. Cream butter and sugar together in a bowl until pale and thick. Separate 5 eggs and add the yolks and the remaining 3 whole eggs, one at a time, into the creamed mixture. Combine baking powder, ground almonds and coconut, then fold into the batter. Whisk egg whites to a soft peak and fold into batter in thirds, alternating with crushed pineapple.

Gently spoon batter into prepared cake tin and cook for 1½ hours until just cooked. Refrigerate for 2–3 hours before serving, as this cake is very moist and it can be a little tricky to handle while warm. Once cake is completely cool, remove from cake tin, slice and serve with a scoop of coconut and lime sorbet and a little extra crushed pineapple, if desired.

coconut and lime sorbet

3 x 400 ml cans good-quality coconut cream

350 g light palm sugar, crushed

zest and juice of 6 limes

makes 1½ litres

Place coconut cream and palm sugar in a medium-sized heavy-based saucepan and warm over a medium heat. Stir until sugar is dissolved, then remove from heat, cool and add lime zest and juice.

Churn in an ice cream machine according to manufacturer's instructions.

Everyone needs a good chocolate brownie recipe ...

gluten-free chocolate brownies

2 cups caster sugar

¾ cup cocoa powder

½ cup rice flour

1 tsp baking powder

4 free-range eggs, beaten

250 g unsalted butter, melted

2 tsp vanilla extract

200 g dark chocolate, chopped

icing sugar, to dust

whipped cream, to serve

serves 8

Preheat oven to 160°C. Line a 22 cm square tin with baking paper. Place all but last two ingredients in a mixing bowl and mix on low speed for 30 seconds before mixing for a further minute on medium to high speed. Spoon mixture into prepared tin and bake for 40–45 minutes or until just set. Remove from oven and allow to cool completely before slicing into squares, dusting with icing sugar, and serving with whipped cream.

This is a great way to celebrate strawberries when they are at their best.

strawberry almond tart

250 g unsalted butter

250 g caster sugar

250 g ground almonds

4 free-range eggs

1 tsp vanilla essence

50 g plain flour

1 recipe sweet short crust pastry, blind baked (see page 192)

1 kg strawberries, hulled and cut in half

1/3 cup vanilla sugar syrup (see below)

cream or vanilla ice cream, to serve

serves 10

Preheat oven to 160°C. Beat butter, sugar and almonds in a mixing bowl until well combined. Add eggs, one at a time, until well incorporated, then add vanilla essence and flour and mix well. Spread frangipane mixture over cooked pastry base with a spatula and bake for 45–50 minutes or until golden brown and just set.

Remove from oven and allow to cool before removing from tin. Place strawberries in a bowl with the vanilla sugar syrup. Lightly toss together and place on top of the frangipane tart. Serve immediately with cream or vanilla ice cream.

vanilla sugar syrup

1 cup caster sugar

3/4 cup water

1/2 tsp vanilla bean paste

makes 1 cup

Place all ingredients in a small saucepan and bring to the boil over a medium to high heat. Remove from heat and allow to cool completely before use.

Store sugar syrup in an airtight container for up to one month.

One of the most asked-for recipes, this intense blackcurrant shortcake is definitely addictive.

blackcurrant shortcake

250 g unsalted butter

250 g caster sugar

2 large free-range eggs

370 g plain flour, sifted

2 tsp baking powder

750 g blackcurrants, stalks removed

1 cup icing sugar

2½ tbsp cornflour

1 tbsp vanilla essence

3 tbsp caster sugar, to dust

cream or ice cream, to serve

serves 10

Preheat oven to 170°C. Grease and line a 28 cm fluted tart tin with removable base with baking paper.

To make shortcake pastry, cream butter and sugar in a mixing bowl until light and fluffy. Add eggs, one at a time, and mix well before adding flour and baking powder. Mix until combined and turn out onto a well-floured bench. Gently knead mixture to form a soft dough, dusting with a little extra flour, if required. Divide into two pieces and roll out each half between two sheets of plastic wrap to make a circle 30 cm in diameter. Place each pastry sheet in the refrigerator for 5 minutes to firm up.

Remove one sheet of pastry from refrigerator and discard bottom layer of plastic wrap before lining the bottom of the tin. Mix blackcurrants, icing sugar, cornflour and vanilla in a bowl. Remove top layer of plastic wrap from pastry and spoon fruit mixture on top. Remove second sheet of pastry from refrigerator, discard plastic wrap and place on top of the tart. Press down lightly on the edges to seal pastry together. Remove excess pastry hanging over the sides of the tin, lightly brush tart top with water and dust with caster sugar.

Place in oven and bake for 1 hour or until pastry is a deep golden brown. Remove from oven and allow to cool completely before serving with cream or ice cream.

slow-cooked carrot cake

380 g plain flour

3 tsp baking soda

1½ tsp table salt

3 tsp mixed spice

1 tsp ground cinnamon

6 free-range eggs

250 g soft brown sugar

450 g white sugar

450 ml sunflower oil

300 g carrots, peeled and grated

100 g walnut pieces

100 g whole natural almonds, roughly chopped

200 g crushed pineapple (unsweetened)

cream cheese icing (see below)

whipped cream, to serve

serves 10

Preheat oven to 150°C. Lightly grease and line a 28 cm round cake tin with removable base with baking paper. Place all but last two ingredients in a mixing bowl and beat on slow speed for 1 minute. Increase speed to medium to high for 2–3 minutes. Pour batter into prepared cake tin. Place in oven and cook for 1¾ hours or until skewer or knife comes out clean. Remove from oven and allow to cool completely before icing with cream cheese icing. Serve with whipped cream.

cream cheese icing

150 g cream cheese

150 g unsalted butter, softened

2¼ cups icing sugar

zest of 1 lemon

Place all ingredients in a mixing bowl and beat on medium to high speed for 3–4 minutes until pale and fluffy.

chocolate and caramel meringue tartlets

1 recipe sweet short crust pastry
(see page 192)

1 cup caster sugar

½ cup water

50 g cold unsalted butter, cubed

½ tsp sea salt

¼ cup cream

1 recipe meringue (see below)

½ cup chocolate ganache (see page 209)

makes 6

Preheat oven to 180°C. Unwrap and slice pastry thinly and press evenly into six 10 cm fluted tart tins with removable bases. Place a piece of baking paper over each tart case and fill with baking beans. Bake for 15 minutes or until golden brown. Remove from oven and allow to cool completely before discarding baking beans and paper and removing cases from tart tins.

To make caramel, place sugar and water in a medium-sized saucepan and bring to the boil over a high heat. Continue to boil until water has evaporated and sugar begins to turn a dark golden colour. Carefully add butter and salt and whisk into caramel, avoiding the resulting steam. Whisk in cream and continue to cook until caramel is thick and rich. Remove from heat and pour 2 tbsp caramel into each tart case. Make meringue and pipe small peaks onto each tartlet. Using a gas torch or oven grill, lightly colour meringue. Warm ganache, drizzle over tartlets and serve immediately.

meringue

200 g caster sugar

100 ml water

100 g free-range egg whites

Place caster sugar and water in a small pot and bring to the boil over a high heat. When sugar syrup reaches 116°C (use a heatproof thermometer to test temperature), whisk egg whites with an electric mixer until soft peaks begin to form. When sugar syrup reaches 125°C, remove from heat and carefully pour down the inside of the mixing bowl into egg whites while mixer is still whisking. Continue to whisk until bottom of the mixing bowl is cool to the touch. For best results, use meringue immediately.

A good fruitcake stands the test of time and Janet's is definitely one of them.

Janet Shand's blue-ribbon fruitcake

day 1

500 g unsalted butter

1 tsp baking soda

2 kg mixed dried fruits

500 g soft brown sugar

1 cup water

1 cup dark rum

¼ tsp salt

1 heaped tbsp golden syrup

Place all ingredients in a large heavy-based pot and warm over a medium heat until butter is melted and sugar is dissolved. Remove from heat and leave at room temperature overnight to allow fruit to soften and flavours to infuse.

day 2

10 free-range eggs

800 g plain flour

2 tsp baking powder

2 heaped tsp mixed spice

¼ tsp salt

makes 1 x 30 cm square cake

Preheat oven to 100°C. Grease and line a 30 cm square cake tin with baking paper. Beat eggs in a mixing bowl until trebled in size. Sift remaining dry ingredients into a separate bowl. Add beaten eggs to fruit mix in three parts, alternating with sifted dry ingredients and taking care not to over-mix. Pour into prepared cake tin and bake for 5–6 hours. Place an ovenproof cup filled with water in the oven while cake is cooking. Cake is ready when skewer or knife comes out clean.

My wife loves a great doughnut and this recipe definitely ticks all the boxes.

easy doughnuts

4 tsp active dry yeast

8 free-range egg yolks

110 g caster sugar

410 ml pouring cream

600 g plain flour

3 litres canola or sunflower oil

vanilla sugar, to dust (see below)

makes 15 doughnuts

Dissolve yeast in ⅓ cup lukewarm water. Whisk yolks and sugar together in a stainless steel bowl for 5 minutes until pale and thick. Add cream, flour and yeast mixture and mix briefly to combine. Cover with plastic wrap and prove at room temperature for 1 hour or until doubled in size.

Lightly dust a clean bench top with flour and turn dough out onto the bench. Lightly dust the top of the dough with a little more flour and gently roll out until 8–10 mm thick. Cut out doughnut shapes using a 7 cm round cutter and place on a lightly floured tray. Cover with a tea towel and prove for a further 30 minutes.

Heat oil in a large pot over a medium to high heat until it reaches 160°C. Cook doughnuts in batches until golden brown on both sides. Remove with a slotted spoon and drain on absorbent kitchen paper. Toss each doughnut in a bowl with a little vanilla sugar and serve immediately.

TIP
To prevent any accidents when deep-frying, use a pot that holds at least twice as much as the amount of oil as you intend to use.

vanilla sugar

2 cups caster sugar

1 tsp vanilla bean paste

makes 2 cups

Mix sugar and vanilla paste together until vanilla seeds are evenly mixed through. Place in an airtight container and store indefinitely. Alternatively, place 3–4 leftover vanilla beans in an airtight container with 2 cups caster sugar and store for one week before using. This allows the aroma to infuse into the sugar.

Great as a tin-filler or as after-dinner petits fours.

burnt butter biscuits

250 g sugar

2 large free-range eggs

1 tsp vanilla extract

250 g unsalted butter

320 g plain flour

4 tsp baking powder

makes 36 biscuits

Preheat oven to 170°C. Line an oven tray with baking paper. Beat sugar, eggs and vanilla in a mixer until pale and thick. Meanwhile, heat butter in a saucepan until frothy and turning golden. Continue to cook until butter begins to burn. (This is important, as most of the biscuits' flavour is developed through this process.) Once butter has started to burn, slowly pour into mixing bowl while the mixer is still running.

Once butter is fully incorporated, sift flour and baking powder together and mix into the creamed mixture until just combined. Roll dough (about 1 dessertspoon) into balls and place on prepared oven tray, allowing plenty of room to spread. Bake for 15–20 minutes or until golden brown. Remove from oven and allow to cool before serving.

Fresh nougat is a real treat and is also surprisingly easy to make.

pistachio and sour cherry nougat

4 sheets rice paper

400 g caster sugar

100 ml liquid honey

200 g liquid glucose

100 ml water

3 free-range egg whites

400 g pistachios, lightly roasted and crushed

200 g dried sour cherries

makes 50 pieces

Lightly spray a 20 cm x 30 cm baking tray and line with 2 sheets rice paper, side by side. Place sugar, honey, glucose and the water in a medium-sized saucepan and bring to the boil over a high heat. Place egg whites in the bowl of an electric mixer, ready for use. When sugar mixture reaches 118°C (use a heatproof thermometer to check the temperature), start whisking egg whites on medium to high speed. When sugar syrup reaches 142°C, remove from heat and slowly pour down the side of the mixing bowl while egg whites are still whisking. (Try to avoid pouring syrup directly onto the whisk attachment to limit the mess.) Turn off machine, remove whisk and fold in pistachios and sour cherries. Turn nougat out into prepared baking tray and spread out evenly. Cover with remaining sheets of rice paper and press down gently to even out mixture. Refrigerate until cold before removing from tray and cutting with a hot, wet, sharp knife into 4 cm x 3 cm pieces.

Store in an airtight container in the refrigerator for up to one week, or in the freezer indefinitely.

everyday basics

sourdough bread

1¼ cups sourdough starter
(see page 190)

7 cups strong baker's flour

2¼ cups tepid (36°C) water

½ cup wheat germ

4 tsp sea salt

vegetable oil, to grease

makes 2 x 450 g loaves

DAY 1

Place sourdough starter, flour, water and wheat germ in the bowl of an electric mixer and mix with a dough hook attachment on low speed for 5 minutes. Turn off machine and leave dough to rest in the bowl for 15 minutes before adding salt and mixing on low speed for a further 5 minutes. Remove dough from mixing bowl and place in a large stainless steel bowl, lightly greased with a little vegetable oil. Cover with plastic wrap and allow to prove in a warm place for 3 hours.

Remove dough from bowl, divide in half and knock back by picking up each half and slapping down onto a bench top 3–4 times. Cover dough on bench top with a tea towel and rest for 15 minutes before kneading and shaping each half into a ball. Lightly flour two round cane banneton baskets or medium-sized bowls and place shaped balls of dough, smooth-side down, in baskets or bowls. Pinch dough together so that there are no loose seams facing upwards. Put baskets or bowls on an oven tray and place both in a large, clean rubbish bag. Leave to prove at room temperature for 1 hour before placing in the refrigerator overnight.

DAY 2

Preheat oven to 220°C. Take bread out of refrigerator and remove rubbish bag. Cover with a tea towel and allow to prove in a warm place for a further 2 hours. Tip bread gently out onto two lightly floured baking trays. Using an old-fashioned razor blade, make a large C-shaped cut in the top of the loaves, about 1 cm deep. Place in oven and bake for 40 minutes until dark brown. Remove from oven and allow to cool for at least 30 minutes before slicing.

sourdough starter

1 litre lukewarm water

500 g strong baker's flour

450 g spray-free grapes

1 cup strong baker's flour

1 cup water

first feed (morning)

2 cups starter

1 cup water

1¼ cup strong baker's flour

second feed (mid-afternoon)

2 cups water

2½ cups strong baker's flour

third feed (early evening)

4 cups water

5 cups strong baker's flour

DAY 1

Mix water and flour together well in a very clean bucket with lid. Wrap up grapes in a large square of muslin and tie off ends with string. Push grape bag into the bottom of the flour and water. Cover bucket with a plastic lid and leave for three days at room temperature.

DAY 4

On the fourth day, feed starter by adding flour and water. Mix well, replace lid and leave starter to ferment at room temperature for a further five days.

DAY 9

Remove grape bag from starter, squeezing out as much juice from the bag as possible. For the next five days, feed starter three times a day as per schedule on left. Mix well with your hands each time it is fed. The first feed each day should be no later than 15 hours after the previous evening's third feed. After five days of feeding, your sourdough starter is ready for use. Repeat feeding schedule each day to maintain starter.

flatbread

2½ cups plain flour
½ tsp salt
1 tbsp olive oil
lukewarm water
extra plain flour, to dust

makes 20 flatbreads

Preheat oven to 180°C. Place the first three ingredients in a large bowl and mix with just enough lukewarm water to make a soft dough. Cover with a tea towel and rest for 45 minutes before dividing into 20 pieces and rolling into small balls. Squash dough into rough circles with your fingers, liberally dust with flour on both sides and roll out with a rolling pin on a well-floured bench top as thinly as you can. Repeat with remaining dough. Roll out each piece of dough again, starting with the pieces that have rested the longest, to 1–2 mm thick. Keep flatbread well dusted with flour to avoid sticking together. Place finished flatbread on oven trays and bake for 2–3 minutes. Remove from oven and cover with a tea towel to keep warm until ready to serve.

savoury short crust pastry

150 g unsalted butter
300 g plain flour
1 pinch salt
chilled water

makes 1 x 28 cm pastry case

Preheat oven to 180°C. Rub butter into the flour and salt. Add just enough water and work together until a soft dough is formed. Roll dough out on a lightly floured bench top until 3–4 mm thick. Gently roll dough onto the rolling pin and unroll again onto an oven tray. Refrigerate pastry for 10 minutes, then remove from refrigerator and drape over a baking paper-lined 28 cm (round) x 4 cm (high) tart tin. Gently mould pastry into the tart tin and cover with a layer of baking paper. Fill with baking beans and blind bake for 15–20 minutes or until golden brown. Allow to cool before removing beans.

TIP
Crumple baking paper into a ball before placing over pastry base and covering with baking beans. This allows the paper to evenly cover the base.

sweet short crust pastry

175 g unsalted butter,
at room temperature

75 g icing sugar

2 free-range egg yolks

250 g plain flour

1 tbsp cold water

makes 1 x 28 cm pastry case

Cream butter and icing sugar in a bowl until light and pale. Add egg yolks, one at a time, mixing well. Mix in flour and just enough cold water to bring the pastry together. Knead lightly, roll into a ball, cover with plastic wrap and refrigerate for 30 minutes or overnight.

Preheat oven to 180°C. Line the base of a 28 cm fluted tart tin with removable base with baking paper. Unwrap pastry, slice thinly and press into tart tin. Ensure pastry is evenly and thinly spread, about 2 mm thick. Remove excess pastry from around edges. Refrigerate pastry base for 10 minutes before lining with a sheet of baking paper. Fill with baking beans and blind bake for 15–20 minutes or until golden brown. Allow to cool before removing beans.

almond short crust pastry

150 g unsalted butter,
at room temperature

60 g icing sugar

30 g caster sugar

30 g ground almonds

½ tsp salt

1 free-range egg

250 g plain flour

makes 1 x 28 cm tart case

Cream butter, icing sugar and caster sugar in a food processor until well combined. Add almonds, salt and egg and continue to blend until well incorporated. Add flour and process until just mixed in. Turn pastry out onto bench top and gently work into a ball. Cover with plastic wrap and refrigerate for at least 30 minutes before using. Remove pastry from refrigerator and bring to room temperature before rolling out into a 30 cm circle between two sheets of plastic wrap.

Preheat oven to 180°C. Line the base of a 28 cm round tart tin with baking paper. Remove plastic from pastry and gently press pastry into the sides of the tin. Cover with baking paper, fill with baking beans and chill pastry in refrigerator for 15 minutes. Blind bake for 15–20 minutes or until pastry is golden brown. Remove from oven and allow to cool completely before removing baking beans and paper.

puff pastry

125 g strong baker's flour
100 g unsalted butter, softened
90 ml water, chilled

makes 300 g

Place flour and 20 g butter in a food processor and blend until combined. With machine still running, add water and blend until a soft dough is formed. Turn pastry out onto a lightly floured bench top and roll out into a 20 cm circle. Using a spatula, spread remaining butter over pastry, leaving a 4 cm unbuttered border around the edges. Fold left and right sides of the pastry round into the centre, overlapping by 2–3 cm and press down lightly on the overlap. Fold bottom and top of pastry round into the centre, again overlapping by 2–3 cm and pressing down in the centre. Lightly flour pastry rectangle and gently roll out to 1 cm thick, maintaining the shape as you do so. Fold left and right sides into the centre to meet, then fold left side completely over to the right side. Cover with a clean tea towel, place on a floured baking tray and refrigerate for 10 minutes to allow pastry to rest.

Remove pastry from refrigerator and repeat rolling and folding process twice more, cover in plastic wrap and reserve for later use.

pie base pastry

200 g plain flour
60 g unsalted butter, chilled and cut into cubes
90 ml milk
5 g salt

makes 300 g

Place flour and butter in a food processor and blend until butter is rubbed into flour. Add milk and salt and pulse until a soft dough starts to form. Remove pastry and knead on a lightly floured bench top to form a smooth dough. Cover dough with plastic wrap and allow to rest at room temperature for at least 30 minutes before use.

fresh pappardelle

250 g strong flour

2 medium-sized free-range eggs

3 medium-sized free-range
egg yolks

1 large pinch salt

1 cup fine semolina flour,
plus extra for dusting

serves 4

Place flour, whole eggs, yolks and salt in a food processor and blend until a firm dough starts to come together. Turn dough out onto a clean bench top and knead together until smooth. Cover dough in plastic wrap and rest in the refrigerator for 30 minutes.

Remove from refrigerator, unwrap and cut dough into eight pieces. Flatten dough pieces with fingers and fold in half. Flatten and fold again. Flatten dough a final time to 4–5 mm thick and pass each piece through a pasta sheet roller on the widest setting. Fold dough in half and pass through roller again on the same setting. Adjust roller setting to 1 and pass each piece through in the same way. Continue to pass dough sheets through roller, adjusting setting after each run. Once dough has passed through setting 7, place each sheet on a lightly semolina-floured bench. Lightly dust pasta with a little more semolina flour, then fold each sheet in half, then half again, lengthways. Cut folded pasta into 2 cm strips horizontally and then toss gently on the bench to separate pasta ribbons. Toss ribbons in remaining semolina flour to prevent from sticking and place on a baking paper-lined tray. Wrap in plastic wrap and store until ready to use.

Fresh pasta is best cooked and eaten on the same day.

potato gnocchi

500 g Agria potatoes

salt and pepper

ground nutmeg, to taste

½ free-range egg, beaten

25 g ground Parmesan

75 g strong flour

serves 4

Wash and boil potatoes, with skins on, until just cooked. Drain and peel with a paring knife while still hot. Mash or pass potatoes through a mouli into a large bowl and make a well in the centre. Season with a little salt, pepper and nutmeg, then add egg, Parmesan and flour and mix together lightly to form a soft dough. Turn out gnocchi dough onto a lightly floured bench top. Divide dough in half and roll out into two 2 cm-thick lengths. Dust with flour and cut dough on the angle into 3 cm lengths, using a sharp knife or dough scraper.

Cook gnocchi in small batches in a large pot of salted boiling water. The gnocchi will sink initially, then rise to the surface when almost cooked. Cook for 1 minute after gnocchi rises and remove with a slotted spoon. Chill in iced water. Remove gnocchi, drain and toss in olive oil to prevent them sticking together. Refrigerate in an airtight container until ready to use.

Gnocchi will keep for up to three days.

wet polenta

350 ml full cream milk

35 g polenta

1 tbsp unsalted butter

2 tbsp ground Parmesan

salt and pepper

makes 400 g

Bring milk to the boil in a small saucepan over a medium to low heat. Pour into a stainless steel bowl and place over a pot of boiling water. Add polenta and whisk occasionally for 2–3 minutes until grains start to thicken. Cover with plastic wrap and cook for 15–20 minutes or until grains are soft. Whisk in butter and Parmesan and season to taste with a little salt and pepper.

mashed potatoes

500 g Agria potatoes, peeled and quartered

1 pinch salt

100 g unsalted butter, chilled and chopped

fresh nutmeg, grated

salt and pepper

serves 4

Place potatoes in a medium-sized pot and cover with cold water. Add a generous pinch of salt and bring to the boil. Reduce heat and simmer until cooked. Drain well, then mash potatoes before folding in butter and seasoning to taste with nutmeg, salt and pepper.

mayonnaise

2 free-range egg yolks

2 tsp Dijon mustard

¼ clove garlic, peeled

juice of 1 lemon

400 ml canola oil

100 ml olive oil

salt and pepper

makes 500 ml

Place egg yolks, mustard, garlic and lemon juice in a food processor and blend. While blending, slowly add canola oil and then olive oil until a thick mayonnaise is formed. Season to taste with a little salt and pepper, and adjust with a little hot water to thin, if necessary.

sweet chilli sauce

10 red chillies, seeds removed
and roughly chopped

4 heads garlic, peeled

3 cups water

200 g palm sugar, crushed

3 tbsp fish sauce

juice of 3 limes

makes 1½ cups

Place chilli and garlic in a small pot with the water and bring to the boil over a medium heat. Reduce temperature, add palm sugar and simmer until chilli and garlic are soft. Remove from heat and blend in a food processor until smooth. Pour chilli sauce into a small bowl and stir in fish sauce and lime juice. Season to taste with a little more fish sauce. Add a little more water if chilli sauce is too hot.

Store in an airtight container in the refrigerator for up to three weeks.

salsa rossa

60 ml olive oil

4 cloves garlic, peeled
and finely sliced

2 tsp sweet smoked
Spanish paprika

2 x 400 g cans chopped
Italian tomatoes

1 tsp caster sugar

salt and pepper

makes 2 cups

Heat olive oil in a medium-sized heavy-based pot over a medium heat. Add garlic and cook for 20 seconds, without colouring, before adding paprika. Cook for a further 10 seconds before adding tomatoes. Bring to the boil, then reduce heat slightly and simmer for 10–15 minutes until tomatoes have cooked out and the sauce has thickened. Add sugar and season to taste with a little salt and pepper. Remove from heat and allow to cool before refrigerating in an airtight container for up to one week.

hummus

2 cups dried chickpeas,
soaked in cold water overnight

1 head garlic

2 cloves garlic, peeled

125 ml olive oil

2 tbsp tahini paste

juice of 1 large lemon

salt and pepper

makes 3 cups

Drain chickpeas and place in a large pot. Cover with cold water. Cut the head of garlic in half and place in the pot with chickpeas. Bring to the boil over a medium to high heat, reduce temperature and simmer for 1 hour or until chickpeas are very tender, topping up with extra water if required. Remove chickpeas from heat and allow to cool in cooking liquor before draining and rinsing under cold running water.

Place cooked chickpeas in a food processor and squeeze out garlic from the two cooked halves. Add raw garlic, olive oil, tahini paste and lemon juice and blend to a smooth paste. Adjust consistency with water as desired and season to taste with a little salt and pepper. (When serving with meat or fish, hummus is best made thinner in consistency.)

Store hummus in an airtight container in the refrigerator for up to one week.

homemade butter

500 ml cream

½ tsp salt

makes 200 g

Place cream in the bowl of an electric mixer and whisk on high speed until it begins to split. Reduce speed to medium and continue to whisk until cream is fully separated into butter and buttermilk. Pour off buttermilk and knead butter under cold running water for 1 minute to remove any remaining buttermilk. Dry butter in a clean, lint-free tea towel and pat between 2 wooden butter pats to remove any excess water. Add salt and mix well to evenly combine. Shape into a block, wrap in greaseproof paper and refrigerate until ready to use.

Butter will keep for one week.

wild elderberry jelly

2 kg elderberries, picked from stalks

2 kg wild apples, cores and skin intact, roughly chopped

water

2–3 kg white sugar

makes 8 x 300 ml jars

Place elderberries and apples in a large heavy-based pot. Cover with water and bring to the boil over a high heat. Reduce temperature and simmer until fruit is soft and pulpy. Remove from heat and ladle fruit and liquid into a clean pillow case over a large pot or bucket. Tie pillow case closed with a piece of strong string and hang over a bucket overnight, using a broom handle placed between the top steps of an open stepladder. (Be sure to suspend bag well above any liquid that initially strains through, so that there is plenty of room for further liquid to drip through overnight.)

The following day, discard contents of pillow case and measure strained liquid into a large heavy-based pot. Bring liquid to the boil over a high heat. Measure out the same quantity of sugar as liquid, add to pot and return to the boil. Continue to boil rapidly for 10–15 minutes or until jelly reaches setting point. Check setting point by spooning a little of the jelly onto a chilled plate and placing in the refrigerator. Once jelly on the plate is cool, run your finger through the middle of it. If it is set, a line will be left through the jelly on the plate. Once jelly has reached setting point, ladle off any foam that may have formed and bottle in sterilized jars while hot.

Keep in a cool, dark place for up to one year.

lemon wholegrain mustard dressing

juice of ½ lemon

¼ cup olive oil

½ cup canola oil

2 tsp wholegrain mustard

2 pinches sea salt

1 pinch black pepper

makes 1 cup

Mix all ingredients together in a small bowl.

Reserve for later use or store in an airtight container in the refrigerator for up to one month.

tamarind dressing

½ tsp shrimp paste

1 x 2 cm knob fresh ginger,
peeled and finely sliced

¼ tsp salt

2 tbsp desiccated coconut, toasted

1 tbsp peanuts, blanched and roasted

2 small red chillies

1 cup palm sugar, crushed

½ cup water

3 tbsp fish sauce

3 tbsp tamarind

makes 1 cup

Preheat oven to 200°C. Wrap shrimp paste in a small piece of aluminium foil and place on a small oven tray with the ginger. (Wrapping shrimp paste in foil will prevent it from burning as it roasts.) Roast for 5–10 minutes or until shrimp paste becomes quite fragrant. Remove from oven and place in a mortar with salt, coconut, peanuts and chillies and grind to a smooth paste.

Place palm sugar and water in a small saucepan and heat until sugar is dissolved and liquid starts to thicken. Add fish sauce and paste and simmer over a medium heat until aromas of the paste are released. Add tamarind and simmer for a further minute before removing from heat. Allow to cool and adjust seasoning with a little more fish sauce, if desired.

Store dressing in an airtight container in the refrigerator for up to one month.

soy, chilli and garlic dressing

6 tbsp sweet soy sauce

4 tbsp oyster sauce

2 tbsp fish sauce

1 large clove garlic,
peeled and crushed

1 red chilli, seeds removed
and finely sliced

1 tsp crushed fresh ginger

makes ¾ cup

Place all ingredients in a bowl and whisk together.

Store dressing in an airtight container for up to two weeks.

chow-chow

800 g onions, peeled and chopped

800 g cucumbers, roughly chopped

800 g green beans, topped and roughly chopped

800 g cauliflower, leaves removed and roughly chopped

800 g green tomatoes, roughly chopped

200 g table salt

1 kg sugar

2 tbsp mustard seeds

2 tsp black pepper, ground

900 ml white vinegar

2 tbsp turmeric powder

2 tbsp dry English mustard

¾ cup cornflour

makes 15 x 300 g jars

Place vegetables in a large pot and cover with water. Sprinkle with table salt and leave overnight.

Strain liquid from vegetables the following day, then add sugar, mustard seeds, black pepper and 600 ml of the vinegar and bring to the boil over a high heat. Reduce heat to a simmer and cook until vegetables are tender. In a small bowl, mix remaining vinegar, turmeric, mustard and cornflour together. Slowly pour the cornflour mixture into the pot, continuing to simmer and stirring until pickle starts to thicken. Add a little more cornflour, mixed with water, to the pickle if a little more thickening is required. Adjust seasoning to taste and bottle immediately in hot, sterilized jars.

Keep in a cool, dark place for up to 1 year.

red onion jam

80 ml olive oil

2 kg red onions, peeled, cores removed and sliced

⅓ cup soft brown sugar

⅓ cup red wine vinegar

1 tbsp fresh thyme leaves, chopped

makes 3 x 300 g jars

Heat olive oil in a heavy-based pot over a medium to high heat. Sweat onions for 10 minutes, stirring occasionally, then add sugar and vinegar. Reduce heat to low and cook for a further hour or until onions are very soft and the cooking juices have reduced to nothing. Mix in thyme and store in sterilized jars.

Refrigerate for up to one month.

pear and walnut chutney

1½ kg ripe, firm pears, peeled,
cored and roughly chopped

250 g cooking apples, peeled,
cored and roughly chopped

250 g brown onions,
peeled and roughly chopped

1 cup cider vinegar

½ cup water

1 cup raisins

zest and juice of 1 orange

2 cups soft brown sugar

1 cup walnut pieces,
lightly toasted

½ tsp ground cinnamon

½ tsp mixed spice

makes 6 x 300 ml jars

Place pears, apples, onions and vinegar in a medium-sized heavy-based pot with the water. Bring to the boil over a medium to high heat, then reduce heat and simmer for 45 minutes until fruit and onions are soft. Add raisins, orange zest and juice and sugar and continue to simmer until liquid has reduced and chutney is thick and rich, stirring often to prevent from catching on the bottom of the pot. Stir in walnuts and spices and spoon chutney into hot, sterilized jars and seal.

Keep in a cool, dark place for up to one year.

confit garlic

15 large heads garlic
2 litres canola oil

Remove excess skin from garlic and slice across the stem end to expose cloves. Place garlic in a small to medium-sized saucepan, cut-side facing upwards, and cover with canola oil. Heat gently over a medium heat until simmering. Cover with a paper cartouche (see page 205) and reduce heat to as low as possible. Cook for 2 hours or until cloves are soft and spreadable. Leave to cool in the oil, then remove and place, cut-side down, on a wire rack to drain for 30 minutes.

Confit garlic will keep for up to three weeks if stored in a sealed container in the refrigerator. Reheat on a baking paper-lined tray in a 200°C oven when required.

hot-smoked salmon

1 x 1.6 kg side of salmon

3 cups soft brown sugar

½ cup table salt

1 litre cold water

1½ cups manuka woodchips

makes 1½ kg

Place salmon, skin-side up, in a long, shallow plastic container with sides at least 5 cm high. To make salmon brine, place sugar, salt and water in a stainless steel bowl and whisk to combine. Pour brine over salmon, cover container with a lid or plastic wrap and refrigerate overnight or for a minimum of 3 hours.

Place a sheet of aluminium foil in the bottom of a small stainless steel box smoker (available at most hardware or camping stores) and sprinkle woodchips evenly over the foil.

Remove salmon from brine and place, skin-side down, on a smoking rack in the smoker. Cover with smoker lid and place over a medium high gas flame or a small outdoor fire. Weigh lid down with a heavy pot or frying pan to prevent smoke from escaping. Smoke for 10–15 minutes until salmon flesh is cooked and firm to the touch.

Remove salmon from smoker and allow to cool before pin-boning, using a pair of tweezers. Turn salmon over, remove skin and store in an airtight container in the refrigerator for up to four days.

Sichuan pepper salt

½ tbsp Sichuan peppercorns

3 tbsp sea salt

makes 2 tablespoons

Heat peppercorns and salt in a heavy-based frying pan over a medium heat until peppercorns become fragrant and begin to pop. Remove from heat and allow to cool slightly before grinding in a spice grinder or with a mortar and pestle.

Store in an airtight container.

jus

4 kg beef soup bones

10 medium brown onions,
skins on and roughly chopped

10 carrots, peeled and
roughly chopped

1 head celery, roughly chopped

6 heads garlic, skins on and
sliced in half

4 leeks, roughly chopped

1 pig's trotter

3 bay leaves

black peppercorns

water, to cover

80 ml canola oil

2 tbsp tomato paste

750 ml red wine

salt and pepper

makes 1 litre

Preheat oven to 200°C. Place beef bones on an oven tray with sides and roast for 1 hour or until as dark as possible without burning. Remove from oven and discard melted fat. Place bones in a large stock pot with half the vegetables. Add pig's trotter, bay leaves and peppercorns and cover with water.

Meanwhile, place 2 cups water in the roasting dish and heat on a stove top over a medium heat. Use a wooden spoon to deglaze the sediment and cooking juices from the bottom of the pan. Pour the liquid into the stock pot and bring to the boil over a high heat. As it comes to the boil, skim any scum from the surface with a ladle and discard. Reduce the heat and simmer for 6–8 hours, skimming as required. Strain stock into another large pot, return to heat and continue to simmer over a low heat.

In a separate pot, heat canola oil over a high heat and add remaining vegetables. Stir often and cook until vegetables are well coloured. Add tomato paste and cook for a further minute before adding red wine. Reduce by half and add to stock. Simmer for 1 hour, then strain through a fine sieve, discarding vegetables. Return to heat and increase temperature until jus comes to a slow, rolling boil. Reduce by four-fifths, skimming as required, until jus begins to coat the back of a spoon. Remove from heat and season to taste.

Store in the refrigerator for up to three weeks. Jus can also be frozen in small containers for several months.

chicken stock

1 free-range chicken carcass

1 brown onion, quartered

1 head garlic, cut in half

1 medium carrot, roughly chopped

1 stalk celery, roughly chopped

5 peppercorns

1 bay leaf

1 sprig fresh thyme

2 stalks parsley

makes 2 litres

Place all ingredients in a large stock pot, cover with cold water and bring to the boil. Reduce heat and simmer for 2 hours, skimming off any scum or fat that rises to the surface with a ladle. Strain and cool stock before refrigerating.

Stock keeps for one week in the refrigerator or three months in the freezer.

to make a cartouche

A cartouche is a paper lid that sits directly on top of food or liquid to prevent it drying out or forming a skin. To make a simple cartouche, take a square piece of baking paper, fold in half, then half again. Fold again to form a triangle and then fold once more, in the same direction, to form another triangle. (The second triangle will resemble a paper dart and the sides will not meet. Don't worry!)

Place the longest point of the triangle at the centre of the pot and cut the cartouche where it meets the rim. The trimmed cartouche will now fit snugly inside the pot.

pistachio tuilles

2 free-range egg whites

60 g caster sugar

15 g plain flour

60 g ground almonds

2 tsp peanut oil

2 tbsp pistachios, crushed

makes 12 tuilles

Preheat oven to 170°C. Line an oven tray with baking paper. Place egg whites, sugar, flour, almonds and peanut oil in a food processor and blend until smooth. From a plastic ice cream container lid, cut out a 6–7 cm circle, discarding the centre piece and trimming off the raised edges. Spread a thin layer of tuille paste on the prepared oven tray using the plastic stencil. Repeat until you have 12 circles of tuille paste. Sprinkle with pistachios and bake until tuilles begin to turn golden brown. Remove from oven and place, pistachio-side down, on a rolling pin while still hot. Once cool, remove tuilles from rolling pin and store in an airtight container for up to one week.

rum and raisin ice cream

1½ cups raisins

¾ cup dark rum

1 litre cream

250 g caster sugar

12 free-range egg yolks

makes 1.5 litres

Soak raisins in rum in a small bowl overnight. Place cream and half the caster sugar in a medium-sized saucepan. Bring to the boil over a medium heat. Meanwhile, in a separate bowl, whisk egg yolks and remaining sugar until light and pale. As the cream comes to the boil, remove from heat and whisk into egg and sugar mixture, combining well. Return ice cream base back to the saucepan and heat to 80°C (use a heatproof thermometer to test the temperature), stirring continuously. Remove from the heat and chill over a bowl of ice.

Once completely cool, churn in an ice cream machine as per manufacturer's instructions. When ice cream is almost finished churning, add raisins and rum and churn for 4–5 more turns until mixed through.

vanilla bean ice cream

1 litre cream

250 g caster sugar

1 vanilla bean, sliced in half
lengthways and seeds scraped

12 free-range egg yolks

makes 1.5 litres

Place cream, half the caster sugar and the vanilla bean and seeds in a medium-sized saucepan. Bring to the boil over a medium heat. Meanwhile, in a separate bowl, whisk egg yolks and remaining sugar until light and pale. As the cream comes to the boil, remove from heat and whisk into egg and sugar mixture, combining well. Return ice cream base back to the saucepan and heat to 80°C (use a heatproof thermometer to test the temperature), stirring continuously. Remove from the heat and chill over a bowl of ice.

Once completely cool, churn in an ice cream machine as per manufacturer's instructions.

honeycomb ice cream

1 litre cream

250 g caster sugar

12 free-range egg yolks

2 cups honeycomb,
lightly shattered (see page 208)

makes 1.6 litres

Place cream and half the caster sugar into a medium-sized saucepan and bring to the boil over a medium heat. Meanwhile, in a separate bowl, whisk egg yolks and remaining sugar until light and pale. As the cream comes to the boil, remove from heat and whisk into the egg and sugar mixture and combine well. Return ice cream base to the saucepan and heat to 80°C, stirring continuously (use a heatproof thermometer to test the temperature). Remove from the heat and chill over a bowl of ice.

Once completely cool, churn in an ice cream machine as per manufacturer's instructions. When ice cream is almost finished churning, add honeycomb and churn for 4 to 5 more turns until mixed through. Freeze as normal.

honeycomb

2 tbsp water

200 g glucose

500 g sugar

1½ tsp baking soda

Heat water, glucose and sugar in a medium-sized saucepan over a high heat until sugar syrup begins to caramelize and turn a light, honey-gold colour. Add baking soda and whisk vigorously, being careful to avoid hot steam as honeycomb expands. Pour immediately onto a baking paper-lined baking tray and allow to cool. Once completely cold, shatter and store in an airtight container at room temperature.

TIP
Pour honeycomb onto a large oven tray, as it expands more rapidly than you might expect!

hazelnut praline

1 cup caster sugar

½ cup water

¾ cup hazelnuts, roasted, with skins removed

Place sugar and water in a small saucepan and bring to the boil over a high heat. Continue boiling until sugar starts to caramelize and turn a deep golden brown. Remove saucepan from the heat and stir hazelnuts into caramel. Pour praline mixture out onto a baking paper-lined oven tray and allow to cool completely before shattering. Store praline in an airtight container for up to two weeks.

vanilla Drambuie syrup

1 cup caster sugar

¾ cup water

½ tsp vanilla bean paste

2 tbsp Drambuie

makes 1½ cups

Place sugar, water and vanilla in a small saucepan and bring to the boil over a medium to high heat. Remove from heat and allow to cool completely. Stir in Drambuie and store in an airtight container for up to one month.

chocolate ganache

250 ml cream

400 g 53% dark chocolate buttons

makes 2 cups

Heat cream in a small saucepan over a medium heat until it just begins to simmer. Remove from heat, add chocolate and stir until smooth. Store in the refrigerator for up to two weeks.

index

Pear Tarte Tatin with Salted Caramel 156

Penne with Broad Beans, Mint and Sole 61

Pheasant, Roast, with Puy Lentils, Red Wine Onions and Baby Carrots 130

Pickled Cucumber 52

Pie Base Pastry 193

Pineapple, Crushed, and Coconut Cake with Coconut and Lime Sorbet 168

Pistachio and Sour Cherry Nougat 186

Pistachio Tuilles 206

Poached Eggs with Hot-smoked Salmon and Homemade Butter 17

Polenta, Wet 195

Pork, Slow-roast Asian, with Salad of Cucumber, Chilli and Soy 122

Potato Gnocchi 195

Potatoes, Mashed 196

Prawn with Chilli, Garlic and Coriander 84

Prawn, Chilli, Coconut and Pumpkin Soup 100

Puff Pastry 193

Pumpkin, Feta and Sage on Crostini 74

Quail, Roast, with Wet Polenta, Cavolo Nero and Salmoriglio 64

Rabbit, Wild, Kebabs with Flatbread and Pear and Walnut Chutney 71

Raspberry Jelly 154

Red Onion Jam 201

Rib-eye of Beef with Roast Kohlrabi and Horseradish 135

Roast Baby Beetroot with Goat's Curd 147

Roast Peaches, Toasted Panettone and Natural Yoghurt 30

Roast Pheasant with Puy Lentils, Red Wine Onions and Baby Carrots 130

Roast Quail with Wet Polenta, Cavolo Nero and Salmoriglio 64

Romanesco Broccoli with Agrodolce 142

Rosewater Meringues 159

Rosewater Syrup 159

Rum and Raisin Ice Cream 206

Salad of Prosciutto, Cherries, Goat's Curd and Vincotto 41

Salads

    Cucumber, Chilli and Soy, with Slow-roast Asian Pork 122

    Edible Flower 144

    Free-range Chicken with Quinoa, Grapes, Basil and Verjuice 37

    Prosciutto, Cherries, Goat's Curd and Vincotto 41

    Red Onion, with Lamb Cutlets, Hummus and Parsley 118

    Shaved Cabbage, with Roast Hazelnuts, Parmesan and Balsamic 150

    Summer Berry, with Milk Gelato 162

    Thai Chicken, with Coconut, Chilli and Roasted Peanuts 48

    Tomato and Basil 139

Salmon, Hot-smoked 203

Salmon, Hot-smoked with Celeriac and Crème Fraiche Soup 93

Salmon, Hot-smoked with Crème Fraîche on Crostini 80

Salmon, Hot-smoked with Poached Eggs and Homemade Butter 17

Salmon, Seared with Avocado Salsa 120

Salmoriglio 64

Salsa Rossa 197

Salted Caramel 156

Savoury Short Crust Pastry 191

Scallops, Seared, with Green Apple, Roasted Macadamia Nuts and Curry Dressing 55

Seared Salmon with Avocado Salsa 120

Seared Scallops with Green Apple, Roasted Macadamia Nuts and Curry Dressing 55

Seared Squid with Pomelo and Tamarind 38

Seared Tuna with Pickled Cucumber and Sesame 52

Seared Venison with Roast Vegetables and Pomegranate Molasses 129

acknowledgements

A huge thank you to everyone who has helped to make this book a reality! To Alison, Antoinette and the team at HarperCollins — thank you for making the whole process so easy and for trusting us! To the wonderful Fiona Andersen — for your bursts of laughter, fabulous family-juggling skills and ever-amazing photography — we are so fortunate to have you as part of the team and can't thank you enough. Thank you to Athena Sommerfeld for her beautiful design. Much appreciation goes to our suppliers who provide us with the superb produce that we love so much. Their commitment to what they do is inspiring! To our gardeners — Mum, Leigh and Cath — for their untiring efforts. Keeping a massive working garden looking so fantastic is no small feat. To our restaurant manager, Sarah, and all our staff — your efforts have made Riverstone Kitchen what it is today and without you we would not have the ability to complete these crazy projects. A heartfelt thank you goes out to our families. To Neil and Dot for your daily support, and to John and Mikki, aka 'Sunshine Coast Book Distribution Centre', your love and encouragement keep us going. Finally, to our loyal customers who share our passion and keep coming back — without you we would not be here and we thank you for the opportunity to do what we love.

Bevan and Monique

HarperCollins*Publishers*

First published in 2012
by HarperCollins*Publishers (New Zealand) Limited*
PO Box 1, Shortland Street, Auckland 1140

Copyright © Bevan Smith 2012

HarperCollins*Publishers*
31 View Road, Glenfield, Auckland 0627, New Zealand
Level 13, 201 Elizabeth Street, Sydney, NSW 2000, Australia
A 53, Sector 57, Noida, UP, India
77–85 Fulham Palace Road, London W6 8JB, United Kingdom
2 Bloor Street East, 20th floor, Toronto, Ontario M4W 1A8, Canada
10 East 53rd Street, New York, NY 10022, USA

National Library of New Zealand Cataloguing-in-Publication Data
Smith, Bevan, 1972-
Riverstone Kitchen : simple / Bevan Smith.
Includes index.
ISBN 978-1-86950-993-4
1. Riverstone Kitchen. 2. Seasonal cooking. 3. Quick and easy
 cooking. I. Riverstone Kitchen. II. Title.
641.564—dc 23

ISBN 978 1 86950 993 4

Publisher: Alison Brook
Design and typesetting by Athena Sommerfeld
Photography by Fiona Andersen

Colour reproduction by Graphic Print Group, South Australia
Printed by RR Donnelley, China, on 157gsm Matt Art